Empaths and Highly Sensitive People

Harnessing the Power of Empathic Abilities
and a Guide for the Highly Sensitive Person

Your Free Gift (only available for a limited time)

Thanks for getting this book! If you want to learn more about various spirituality topics, then join Mari Silva's community and get a free guided meditation MP3 for awakening your third eye. This guided meditation mp3 is designed to open and strengthen ones third eye so you can experience a higher state of consciousness. Simply visit the link below the image to get started.

https://spiritualityspot.com/meditation

Contents

Part 1: Empaths

Unlocking the Hidden Power of Empaths and a Guide to Protecting Yourself Against Energy Vampires and Narcissists

Introduction

Do you feel mentally drained after spending time in public? Do you feel emotionally tired when you are in a crowd? Are you sensitive to the emotions of others? Do you often feel you are different from others? Have you been described as overly sensitive, soft, or even touchy? Are your emotions magnified and intense? If you answered "yes," these are all the signs that you may be an empath.

Empathy is the ability to understand what others are feeling and experiencing. It is a wonderful gift, but being an empath in the modern world is not easy. You are surrounded and exposed to environments and individuals who can overstimulate you. For an empath, this stimulation can be overwhelming. Highly sensitive individuals often struggle to cope with the external stimuli of everyday life. Stimuli, coupled with the energy of others, can make an empath exhausted. Empaths often experience emotional overload, mental fatigue, and even anxiety. Simple daily activities such as commuting to work using public transport or watching television can be challenging for empaths.

The first step is to accept and embrace your gift. Empathy is a strength, not a weakness. Everything falls into place once you take this initial step. After this, it is time to harness your gift and recognize that you are an empath. By appreciating this wonderful gift that you have been blessed with, life will become easier.

In this book, you will learn about the meaning and common traits of empaths, strengths and weaknesses of empaths, and the factors that affect an empath, such as diet and the environment. It includes information about the importance of leading a balanced life and common mistakes empaths must avoid for a happy and healthy life. You will also discover tips to help you maintain healthy and successful relationships, choose the best career options, and the role empaths play in today's world. As an empath, it's important to harness and shield your empathy from the world. By following the simple techniques and tips discussed in this book, you can unlock your empathy powers and protect them from energy vampires and narcissists.

So, are you eager and excited to learn more about this? Do you want to discover the hidden powers of empathy? If you answered "yes" again, it's time to get started without further ado.

Chapter 1: What is an Empath?

The Meaning of Empath, Empathy, and Empathetic

Are you affected by the feelings of the people around you? Do others describe you as empathetic? Perhaps sometimes you have sensed and felt the emotions of those around you— including physical symptoms—as if they were your own? If this sounds familiar, you are probably an empath. This sensitivity is something only one-two percent of the general population is blessed with. Those with empathy often use their intuition and emotions to guide their decision-making instead of relying on logic and rationalism. It is a symbol of personal strength and belief and is certainly a signal of empathy.

Researchers have a keen interest in empathy, but only a few studies ever concentrated on an empath's life. According to science, many believe empaths have hyper-responsive mirror neurons. These are brain cells responsible for the feelings of compassion. Once these mirror neurons are hyperactive, you become hypersensitive to the electromagnetic fields of the brain and heart.

This is perhaps one reason why you are intuitive and deeply feel others' emotions.

Spending time in public or being surrounded by those in pain can make an empath exhausted.

Dopamine is a chemical that triggers feelings of pleasure. Empaths with tendencies of introversion are sensitive to dopamine. Excessive stimulation can overwhelm an empath. The great news is that empaths have the power to reprogram their minds to deal with and avoid unnecessary external stimulation and lead happier lives. Even if you're not introverted, hypersensitivity comes with various side effects, such as emotional overload, exhaustion, depression, and anxiety. An empath can feel these complex emotions when exposed to stressful situations. Unsurprisingly, these mental and emotional symptoms can present themselves as headaches, an elevated heart rate, and a general feeling of fatigue.

These things happen because of an empath's inability to distinguish their feelings, emotions, and pain from those around them. Internalizing one's feelings is difficult. Imagine if you had to deal with a combination of your emotions and others' emotions without being aware of whose emotions you are feeling. This causes extreme internal turmoil, which can present itself as physical symptoms. So, all empaths need to understand and protect their personal energy from others.

Empaths, Introverts, Highly Sensitive Persons, and Narcissists

No two people are alike; everyone is unique. Neurodiversity is responsible for this diversity. People are all wired differently, and this diversity in neural networking determines their unique characteristics. Certain individuals are incapable of concentrating on tasks because of their high energy levels, such as those with ADHD, while others require environmental and social stimulation to stay occupied, such as extroverts. Highly sensitive people, introverts, and empaths lie on the extreme end of the personality spectrum compared to extroverts. Introverts can all be overly stimulated by external stimuli and sensitive to those around them. But there is a difference between introverts, empaths, and highly sensitive individuals. Yes, even though these words have been used synonymously, they are not the same.

Introverts

As mentioned, people react differently to external stimuli. Not many understand what introversion means. Introverts do not detest social events. They just have a different idea of social gatherings, and their approach is different from that of extroverts. This difference stems from a natural biological differentiation, how individuals react to different situations, and their relaxation ideas. Introverts feel overstimulated when engaging in conversations with multiple people. Instead, they prefer having deep and genuine conversations with a few individuals, unlike extroverts, who thrive in crowds. Since their senses are easily stimulated, they tend to get exhausted and overwhelmed when surrounded by several people— unlike extroverts.

These factors are the main reason introverts withdraw from the world and have to take a break and recharge. It is a misconception that introverts do this because of their lack of self-confidence or self-esteem. Instead, it's their way of recharging their personal batteries. It is a natural reaction to excessive pressure and stimulation. For instance, what happens when someone shines a bright light in your eyes? Even if you look at it for just a second, you still turn your face away or close your eyes. Think of this external light as all the stimulation introverts face. Sooner or later, they need to look away!

They do this by withdrawing from the world for a while.

Highly Sensitive People (HSP)

A highly sensitive person differs from an introvert. The only similarity is their extremely low threshold for external stimulation, such as smells, sounds, and lights. HSPs do not enjoy socializing. Just like empaths, even they need solitude to recharge their batteries after a hectic day. The stimulation drains them of their energy and overburdens their internal systems. HSPs can be introverted, but not all introverts are HSPs.

Empaths

Empathy is not restricted to a particular personality type. They can be introverts, extroverts, or even ambiverts. All empaths tend to be highly sensitive, but while all empaths are HSPs, not all HSPs are empaths. Empaths not only feel what others are feeling, but they can also absorb the emotions into their bodies. They display extremely high levels of compassion and empathy for those around them. As with introverts, empaths love to spend time by themselves and need solitude to maintain a sense of balance and control. Their ability to understand what others are going through and their perspective make them natural nurturers and caregivers. They have an undeniable inherent urge to help other people. They are blessed with the gift of understanding and intuition. When these are coupled with compassion, it becomes obvious that they need to help others.

As you can see, many empaths, introverts, and HSPs tend to display overlapping characteristics. The differences that set them apart are minute. One similarity that cannot be overlooked is their extreme sensitivity to external stimuli and the need for alone time to recharge their energy.

Narcissists

If empaths and HSPs lie on one end of the empathetic spectrum, narcissists lie on the other end. People call those who are devoid of empathy narcissists. Everyone knows that opposites attract, and so narcissists are drawn to empaths. A narcissist's lack of empathy draws them to those with high levels of empathy. An empath's loving and nurturing nature prompts them to help a narcissist. Unfortunately, a narcissist's selfish nature only leads to chaos. An empath is giving while a narcissist does not understand the basics of a mutual relationship. It is not just narcissists that empaths need to shield themselves from but all types of energy vampires. You will learn how to do all this in the subsequent chapters.

Empaths and Empathy

Being an empath and being empathetic are two different things. When someone describes themselves as empathetic, it means their heart goes out to others. As an empath, you not only empathize with others, but you also experience their feelings as if they were yours. The compassion you experience for others is because of mirror neurons. The mirror neuron system is hyperactive in an empath, which is why they can absorb others' emotions and physical symptoms into their bodies. At times, differentiating between one's emotions and others' emotions becomes increasingly difficult for an empath.

Empaths experience different types of sensitivities. For instance, physical empaths can experience physical symptoms that others experience and absorb them into their bodies. Their keen sense of understanding makes empaths natural healers. Many empaths are sensitive to others' emotions and pick up on them, regardless of whether they are good or bad, while others are even sensitive to food and display extreme sensitivities to various ingredients.

Empathy is a gift because it increases one's creativity, compassion, and sense of integration. It also makes them feel well connected with those around them and the world. However, living in this stimulated state can be emotionally draining for an empath. Even simple daily interactions can be uncomfortable and a source of stress. Those unaware of their empathic abilities use unhealthy coping mechanisms, like relying on alcohol or drugs or emotional eating to cope with everyday challenges. You will learn more about the strengths and weaknesses of an empath in the following chapters.

Common Traits of Empaths

Empaths are highly sensitive individuals capable of feeling and absorbing the emotions of those around them. This is perhaps a trademark feature of all empaths. Understanding and rationalizing their feelings can become difficult when they need to continue to filter everything they experience. Apart from this, all empaths share common traits. If you think you are an empath, it is highly likely you have the traits discussed in this section.

Highly Sensitive

As discussed in the previous section, empaths are highly sensitive individuals. But there is a difference between a highly sensitive person and an empath. All empaths are sensitive, but all HSPs are not necessarily empaths. If you have ever been told to toughen up or you are extremely sensitive, it's a sign of empathy. Empaths can easily absorb and experience what others are feeling. They are naturally nurturing and will do this irrespective of the circumstances because of their giving nature.

Absorb Emotions of Others

Empaths not only understand what others are experiencing and feel their physical symptoms, but they are also highly attuned to the moods and emotions of others. Empaths can literally feel everything, and it can be extreme at times. This is one reason why they often become exhausted. Absorbing negativity from their surroundings and other difficult emotions such as anger, anxiety, and sadness can quickly overwhelm and drain their inner energy. It's not just negative energy they can absorb, though; they can also absorb positive energy. This is why empaths thrive in an environment filled with happiness, love, and peace. If everyone around them is happy and giving out positive energy, an empath will experience positive feelings too.

Introverted Nature

Since empaths experience everything that others are feeling, they tend to get overwhelmed quickly. This is the reason why most empaths lean toward introversion. Being exposed to extremely stimulating environments is often amplified for an empath, which is why they like being on their own and prefer one-on-one contact or engaging with small groups. Even if an empath is not an introvert, they try to limit their time in public settings.

Highly Intuitive

Intuition is perhaps one of the greatest skills empaths are naturally blessed with. In fact, most life experiences they have are through intuition, as they can see beyond others' facades. It is easy for them to decipher what others are really feeling and experiencing. This is the basis for their intuition, so it is quintessential that empaths listen to their "gut" feelings and improve their intuitive skills.

They Need Me-Time

As mentioned, spending time in a stimulating environment can be draining for an empath. Unsurprisingly, it is why empaths need to take a break from everything that happens in their life to recuperate. If you are an empath, you realize the importance of me-time. You need to spend time by yourself to recharge and reenergize your internal batteries. It also gives you a chance to take a rest from the emotional overload of others.

Empaths have highly tuned senses, and it is not just energy they absorb; noises, sounds, and smells can also be stimulating. Going to a concert might not be an empath's idea of a fun activity. Instead, an empath will more likely enjoy curling up with a book in the comfort of their home. If you have ever experienced these situations in the past, you are probably an empath.

Overwhelmed by Intimacy

Relationships are seldom easy and are difficult for empaths. Imagine being able to experience and feel what others around you are feeling all the time? It is almost like a song you cannot stop humming or get out of your head. Now, spending time in close quarters with another individual for prolonged periods can obviously become draining. This is the reason why empaths are often overwhelmed by intimacy. It does not mean that empaths don't like intimate relationships; they just struggle more than others to maintain relationships. One of the reasons they are scared of intimacy is that they often feel they will lose their identity or are afraid of being engulfed by their partner's emotions. For an empath to be in a relationship, they need to let go of any preconceived notions about individuality and relationships in general. Empaths are super responders, and this factor, coupled with their introverted nature, makes it difficult for them to spend time with others.

Soft Targets for Energy Vampires

Energy vampires and narcissists often look for people who offer unconditional love, support, and acceptance. So, an empath becomes an ideal target for energy vampires. These vampires thrive when they are feeding off the positive energy of those around them. An empath's sensitivity is perhaps the main reason they are drawn to them. Energy vampires such as narcissists lack empathy. As humans, people are often drawn to others who have skills or traits that they don't. Thus, an empath's high levels of compassion and sensitivity make them magnets for energy vampires.

Refuge in Nature

A simple way for an empath to reenergize is by spending time in nature. Whether it is going for a walk or sitting in the garden, simple activities can offer them solace. If you are drawn to nature, especially after an overwhelming or a tough day, it's a sign of empathy.

Always Giving

Because empaths know what others are going through and where they are coming from, it becomes easier for them to understand what others are feeling and experiencing at any given point. So, it is natural that empaths are extremely giving and big-hearted individuals. Regardless of the situation, they always try to soothe any pain or discomfort others feel. After all, if negative energy surrounds them, they tend to feel it too. Perhaps it is a homeless person at an intersection, a crying baby, or a hurt animal—an empath always tries to help. Instead of just helping others by reaching out to them, empaths also tend to absorb others' pain. By depleting their personal energy reserves, they help others. This is the reason why empaths are often giving. Again, this extreme sensitivity they display toward all living beings in their environment and surroundings makes them ideal targets for energy-sucking vampires.

Now that you know the different traits exhibited by empaths, it is time for a little self-introspection. Carefully go through the points discussed in the section, spend time with yourself, and allow your intuition to guide the way. If you notice you have any or all the traits mentioned earlier, chances are you are an empath.

Chapter 2: Empath Strengths

Empathy is a beautiful gift, and the world needs more empaths. Empathy can be the key to the end of all our problems and sufferings. Unfortunately, empaths are often viewed to be weak and powerless. They are labeled as too touchy and oversensitive. If others have told you to toughen up or grow a thick skin, do *not* listen to that advice. Instead of believing your empathy to be a weakness that holds you back, consider it a strength. Yes, empathy is your superpower, and it distinguishes you from all others. Empaths are stronger than others believe.

This section looks at the strength of an empath.

Imagination

Empaths are incredibly imaginative. Since the world of emotions is your primary domain, you can understand and handle them better than any other human being. Your ability to deal with a variety of emotions simultaneously increases your imagination. Instead of allowing your rational mind to guide your decisions, imagination comes into play. Imagination allows you to see the possibilities and opportunities available in any situation that others cannot see. Empaths are quite creative as they are dreamers. They also have the power to turn their dreams into reality. The world is different for others, and you experience it vividly. All empaths have a constant urge to create or build something that helps others. Your imagination and creativity also make it easier to express your thoughts, emotions, and true self. It allows you to view the world and life inversely from those around you. Creativity also helps enhance and strengthen your natural skills and empathy.

Different Perspectives

Your empathy allows you not just to understand what others are feeling but also to experience it. It allows you a better understanding of where the other person is coming from. Instead of allowing superficial reactions to cloud your judgment, it helps you view things from someone else's perspective. An empath does not have to try to place themselves in someone else's shoes consciously. Their empathy allows them to do this naturally. This makes it easier to view things from others' perspectives and also enhances your decision-making skills. It offers you a better understanding of yourself, the individuals you deal with, and the world in general.

Problem-solving Skills

Empaths are blessed with amazing problem-solving skills. Take a moment and think about all the situations when others have approached you in their times of need. Why did they do this? There might have been others they could have approached, but they chose you. Why do you think this happened? It is because they knew you could help them to solve their problems. Your imagination and the ability to view a situation from different perspectives improve your problem-solving skills. Whether it's an argument or a fight, an empath can solve these problems. In a world where the "I am right" attitude exists, conflicts are common. Empathic individuals can be instrumental in conflict resolution and problem-solving. It allows you to understand how different sides perceive reality. You can play the role of an observer and a mediator without being overly attached to either side. By identifying triggers and understanding the hidden meanings behind the words communicated, solving problems becomes easier for an empath.

Heightened Senses

Empaths can absorb and experience the emotions and feelings of those around them, whether negative or positive. For instance, if you spend time with positive individuals and in the company of loved ones, your happiness quotient increases. This heightened sensitivity helps you enjoy the little things in life that are mostly ignored. You don't need any grand gestures to feel happy. Your empathy allows you to stay in the moment and enjoy life the way it is. It gives you a chance to smell the roses and not let life pass you by. Instead, it ensures you enjoy every second of it. Even spending time outdoors can revitalize and reenergize you.

Not Scared Of Being Alone

Most people are scared of being alone. In fact, this is one of the greatest human fears, but empaths thrive when they get alone time. It not only helps them rebalance their lives but also gives them a chance to recuperate. It also increases their self-awareness. Once you learn to be comfortable with yourself, life becomes incredibly simple. When you start spending time with yourself, it makes you aware of your thoughts, emotions, and feelings. It also helps to distinguish your emotions from others. You don't need to be the center of attention to feel good about yourself. Even reading a book at home can be quite comforting.

Accepting Of Change

Change is the only constant in life, and empaths understand this. An empath knows change is unavoidable. Once you accept this, living life becomes simple. Adaptability ensures you can thrive in any situation without letting it become overwhelming. You might not always like the situation you are stuck in, but your empathy ensures you accept the situation and move on. Since you are good at getting a sense of what others want or like, it becomes easier to understand different ways of life. It makes you more accepting and accommodating.

Ability To Accept

Most people view the world from their perspective and are often prejudiced. They might not realize it, but they are. Surprisingly, empaths are immune to this prejudice. They do not assume or generalize when it comes to the feelings of others. They don't label what others are feeling or experiencing. Looking at things from someone else's perspective allows you to perceive what others are feeling. You start thinking of those around you as emotional beings. So, empaths are accepting not just of others, but of life in general.

A great thing about an empath is they understand and accept others the way they are. As an empath, you might be tempted to help others or fix a situation. However, you must realize there is only so much you can do and not to go beyond it. Once you make peace with this realization, life becomes easier. When you accept people the way they are without desiring perfection, forming and maintaining relationships becomes easier. This is a unique trait of an empath that sets them apart from others.

Good Listeners

Empaths are great listeners. In a world where everyone wants to talk, listening has become a lost art. Fortunately, empaths are the best listeners one can get. This is also why people commonly seek out their most empathetic friends or loved ones to talk to when they need a sounding board. Empaths are not scared of making themselves vulnerable and are attentive listeners. These two ingredients make you an incredible person to talk with. You not only understand what others are saying but also their reasons for behaving the way they do. In a life where everyone feels misunderstood, the world needs more empaths. When you make yourself vulnerable to others, it increases their willingness to be open, honest, and vulnerable.

Healthy Curiosity

Humans are naturally curious. Empaths are incredibly curious and inquisitive. As an empath, your curiosity is the primary factor that keeps you interested and engaged in various topics. Curiosity is also an important aspect of enhancing one's life, reducing the chances of loneliness, and improving overall satisfaction. When you are curious, it makes it easier to learn. If you keep learning, you keep growing in life.

Heal Others

Empaths are natural healers. They have a natural tendency to help and heal others. An empath can absorb negative emotions, feelings, or sensations from others and replace them with positivity. As an empath, you have probably done this several times in your life and have not even realized. Once you heal yourself as an empath, helping others becomes incredibly simple. The feeling you experience when you see someone in trouble is your empathy at work. It guides the way and lets you do your best to heal others in any way possible.

Human Lie Detectors

Empaths have a strong sense of intuition that allows them to detect lies easily. You are a human lie detector and can instantly detect when someone is dishonest. Regardless of whether you know them or not, internal alarm bells start ringing whenever someone lies to you. Never ignore this little voice in your head that tells you something is wrong. If your gut says something is wrong, it is highly likely that something is amiss. When you truly know what others feel and can see through their facade, detecting lies becomes easy.

Whatever mask people put on, you can see their true persona because of your empathy. Since you are more aware of others' thoughts, emotions, and feelings, it becomes easy to determine when someone is lying to you. If someone says they are fine, but they are really sad on the inside, you can detect it easily. No one can lie to you without you knowing it. For instance, if you notice that a colleague at work seems a little low, you ask them what happened. They might say everything is fine, but, as an empath, you can see right through this mask and get to the root of the problem. Your ability to detect lies helps you form happy, positive, and successful relationships.

Were you surprised after going through the list of strengths discussed in this chapter? Perhaps these are strengths you never noticed about yourself. Dear empath, you are stronger than you give yourself credit for. Misconceptions others have about empathy or empaths do not define you. Your sensitivity is a brilliant thing. Empathy is a superpower, and empaths are superheroes. They are the superheroes the world desperately needs right now. The simplest way to hone your strength as an empath is to accept your empathy. If you are an empath, you are blessed with a rare gift. Accept it and harness its power.

Before you learn to strengthen and protect your energy as an empath, it is important to understand the wisdom empathy offers. Remind yourself of all these strengths whenever your gift overwhelms you. Now that you understand the strengths, you might find your view of empathy has changed somewhat. It is a gift which you should cherish. Accept and embrace your empathy with open arms, and all your strengths will be magnified. You will learn more about unlocking your true potential as an empath in the subsequent chapters.

Chapter 3: Empath Weaknesses

In the previous chapter, you were introduced to empaths' strengths. Unfortunately, the traits that make them strong can also become their weaknesses. Living in a constantly stimulating environment and the inability to distinguish their emotions from others can be overwhelming. An empath's sensitivity and empathy come at a high cost and are often misunderstood. This section looks at different struggles an empath faces.

Inability to Say "No"

Empaths have a natural desire and an inherent tendency to help those around them. They try to make others happy or feel better regardless of the situation. This desire makes it difficult for them to say "no." As an empath, you probably feel it is your duty and responsibility to help everyone who needs your help. When you start feeling like this, pleasing others becomes the norm. It might make you feel better initially, but in the long run, it gets exhausting. If you keep getting stuck in situations that can be avoided by saying "no," you will be left with no energy. It can also make you feel out of control while increasing your stress levels. Another disadvantage of an empath's inability to say "no" is that others will take them for granted. You end up displeasing yourself when you constantly try to please others.

Television Becomes a Challenge

Television is a source of entertainment for most people. At the end of a tiring day, who wouldn't want to relax and watch TV? But this simple act others enjoy can be challenging for an empath. Since they are finely attuned to others' emotions, regardless of whether the event is happening around them or across the world, empaths can feel it. This means watching a horror movie, an emotional drama, or even the news becomes unbearable.

Susceptibility to Addictions

Dealing with one's emotions is problematic. Imagine if you had to live your life dealing with the emotions, feelings, and experiences of all those around you as well? When an empath cannot deal with their emotions or accept their empathy, living life is typically challenging. This is a reason why empaths always seek an escape. Blocking all the unnecessary emotions and feelings is a self-defense mechanism. This is also a reason why empaths are quite susceptible to addictions. Instead of dealing with their problem, they seek an escape. The simplest escape route is dependence on harmful substances such as alcohol, drugs, tobacco, or any other addictive behavior. In a bid to survive and preserve oneself, an empath develops unhealthy behaviors.

See-Through Others

In the last chapter, it was mentioned that empaths are human lie detectors. They feel and understand what others are saying and can decide whether they are telling the truth. This is an incredibly helpful quality that can be used to navigate human life. But it is quite painful when you know your friend or a loved one is lying to you. It can make you feel like a loner and vulnerable in this big bad world. Even a small white lie told by a loved one can be detected by an empath. Since they are naturally hypersensitive, a small lie hurts a lot. It can also result in distrust of others. After all, if your loved ones lie to you, how can you depend on them? Dealing with these kinds of emotions is exhausting, and it prevents empaths from forming and maintaining healthy and positive relationships in life.

Dealing with Intimacy

As mentioned earlier, a common problem empaths face is intimacy. Every empath needs quiet time. They need to get away from others to recharge their energy. This can make it incredibly difficult for an empath to spend time with the partner. When you spend all your time with another individual, you tend to feel what the other person is feeling as an empath. When your senses are overrun continuously because of this connection, relationships become difficult. When spending time together becomes overwhelming, your need to withdraw from others also increases. In such a situation, an intimate relationship becomes tricky. The universe is made of energy, and energy continually flows from one person to another. An empath connects with another individual, which means they open themselves up, and their energy field is vulnerable. This can overwhelm an empath, overstimulate them, and result in chronic fatigue. Since intimacy can burn out an empath, the possibility of intimacy can seem scary.

When an empath is emotionally invested in their partner, it easily clouds their judgment. This is also one of the reasons why empaths usually get stuck in unhealthy relationships. They are magnets for narcissists and other energy vampires. These kinds of unhealthy relationships drain not only an empath of their empathy but also their energy, and compassion becomes a burden. Caring too much and being unable to shut off this compassion for others can leave you feeling tired and restless. It also makes you feel as if you have no control over your life. These factors can harm any relationship, especially the intimate ones in an empath's life.

Trouble Socializing

Empaths love solitude because it helps them gain a sense of balance in an extremely stimulated world. They have trouble socializing with others around them. If spending too much time in public can drain you of your energy, why would you want to do this? The need to get away from others to recharge their energy and regain control of their emotions is why most empaths lean toward introversion. Their introversion is a self-defense mechanism. Empaths need a lot of alone time. Unfortunately, not everyone can understand this. It can also be quite tricky to explain why you need alone time to others.

As an empath, you might constantly face an inner struggle between wanting to go out and staying in. Empaths need time alone to process their emotions and stop absorbing the emotions of others. This is also the reason why they are misunderstood as introverts. Not all introverts are empaths, and not all empaths are introverts. Striking the right balance between socializing and solitude is not easy. Unless you do this, you cannot lead a happy and well-balanced life.

Tiredness

By now, you have realized that empaths are constantly drained of their energy. If an empath's energy is like a bucket full of water, every emotion or feeling they absorb from others puts a hole in this bucket. The bucket will sooner or later be empty. This is precisely what happens to empaths when they are out in the world. Unless an empath learns to establish and enforce their personal boundaries, empathy can be overwhelming. Emotional fatigue is quite real for empaths. Regardless of whether it is happiness or sadness, every emotion is severely magnified for an empath and surrounded by emotions, and absorbing all these emotions increases one's emotional fatigue.

Taken for Granted

An empath's inability to say "no" and their boundless compassion make them the perfect target for all energy vampires. Empaths are not immune to narcissists and other toxic people. Do your friends and other loved ones approach you when they are feeling low or tired? Have others told you they feel better after spending time with you? This is because of your empathy. As an empath, you end up absorbing all the negative emotions from others and give away your positive energy. After a while, you will be left with nothing and end up becoming a dumping ground for emotional pain. Being taken for granted is seldom pleasant. As this becomes the norm, emotional stress increases. It can also result in anxiety, depression, and isolation.

Depression and Anxiety

It might not be true for all empaths, but it is not uncommon for most of them to struggle with a mental health disorder. Due to their high sensitivity to emotions, they deal with stress and self-doubt. Every negative emotion or feeling an empath absorbs from others is similar to getting hit with a brick. If negative people constantly surround you, you pick up their negative energy. This negativity can fester into mental health conditions such as depression or chronic anxiety. It is not just your problems you need to deal with; you have to deal with others' problems as well. If you live your life feeling like you do not fit in or others don't understand you, it creates a sense of isolation. This isolation can worsen your negative thinking and increase your risk of developing depression or anxiety as an empath.

Empathy comes with pros and cons. Most of the strengths that empaths have can become their weaknesses. This usually happens when they cannot deal with their empathy or have a tough time balancing their emotions.

After going through this list, you might have finally understood why you struggle daily with simple things that others seem to enjoy. This will also help you watch out for situations and individuals you need to avoid to protect yourself. Once you embrace your empathy and learn to harness its power, overcoming these weaknesses becomes incredibly simple. You will learn more about doing this in the subsequent chapters.

Chapter 4: How Diet Affects an Empath

You need to concentrate on three important aspects to live healthily and happily: Sleep, exercise, and diet. A common factor often overlooked is the role that diet plays on mental and physical wellbeing. Unsurprisingly, empaths are more susceptible to diet-related problems. Yes, diet can have a positive or adverse effect on empaths. Food is a source of energy and empaths are incredibly sensitive individuals. Consuming the wrong diet or not eating healthy food can harm an empath's overall wellbeing and empathy.

Why Does Diet Affect Empaths?

You might have realized your rather unique dietary needs—for instance, stimulants such as caffeine or sugar trigger extreme reactions. You might also have accidentally stumbled upon the fact that eating certain foods harms your overall energy levels. Food sensitivities are quite common in empaths and highly sensitive individuals. This section looks at different reasons why diet affects empaths.

Self-Defense Mechanism

As you have already learned, empaths are extremely sensitive to their feelings and the feelings of others, which makes them super sensitive to crowds. They do not like to be ogled, and any form of attention can send their already hyperactive senses into overdrive. Some might find attention flattering and even thrive on it, but for an empath, this merely worsens their energy fields. An empath's body and mind work together to protect themselves from any potential predators. They use food as a coping mechanism. If the said empath experienced any form of sexual abuse or trauma in the past, a self-defense mechanism is weight gain or obesity. How do you feel when you are carrying a few extra pounds? Chances are you don't find yourself quite as attractive. When you feel like this on the inside, you tend to project this energy externally too. This reduces the chances of any unnecessary or unwanted sexual attention from others.

Daily Struggles

How would you feel if you were cramped up into a tight enclosure with hundreds of people? You might feel like a chew toy attacked by a pack of wild dogs. Simple tasks such as commuting to work using public transport can make you feel like the chew toy mentioned above if you are an empath. The day-to-day challenges that empaths face increase their emotional and spiritual turmoil. A simple subway ride can be an excruciating and harrowing experience for empaths. Empaths don't just internalize others' feelings; they tend to feel them as if they were their own. They feel it in their muscles, body, bones, and nerves. This constant onslaught of energies makes them incredibly sensitive and causes much internal turmoil. From this perspective, a little extra weight acts as a natural barrier that shields them from the external energies they don't want to absorb.

Allergies and Disorders

Empaths suffer from a variety of hormonal imbalances, allergies, autoimmune disorders, and even neurological issues. Living in a perpetually hyperactive state of emotions, sensations, and environmental toxins can stress your physical body. This, in turn, sends the immune system into hyperdrive. When your immune system does not function normally or starts attacking itself, it results in allergies and autoimmune disorders. These two conditions are also associated with the diet you consume.

Consuming healthy and wholesome meals instead of processed and refined foods helps restore balance to your physical body. Unless your body and mind are healthy, you cannot maintain your overall health. There is an undeniable relationship between these two things and your food choices matter. Any gluten present in grains such as wheat or barley can result in weight loss or gain in those with coeliac disease. Foods that have inflammatory reactions to allergies can encourage water retention in the body. If you take a moment and think about it, most of the food sensitivities you experience can be due to your inability to deal with all the emotions you experience. Stress is another stimulant that prevents your body from functioning optimally. If your body cannot function optimally, how can your immune system be healthy?

Emotional Eating

When you are feeling down, do you feel like eating something sugary? Do you crave junk food when you feel out of sorts? This is a form of emotional eating. Empaths who have not learned to handle their empathy prevent other energies from overtaking their struggle to lead a balanced life. It can trigger emotional difficulties such as anxiety or depression. During these highly charged emotional times, food is a great outlet. Turning to comfort foods helps soothe their distress. When you are constantly overwhelmed emotionally, physically, and spiritually, it becomes difficult to manage your stress levels.

The simplest way to overcome stress is by accepting your empathy and taking steps to protect your personal energy from others. You will learn more about shielding yourself and harnessing your abilities in the subsequent chapters. For now, take time for self-introspection. Make a note of all the times you have experienced a powerful emotion that made you want to eat. If you do this often, it is a sign that you are not handling your gift of empathy very well.

A Feeling of Alienation

An empath's body image issues are not just about weight gain or loss. Instead, they are associated with the feeling of being alienated from their physical self. When your body becomes a cage that traps all sorts of energies, feelings, and emotions, a feeling of disassociation increases. When you feel dissociated from your body, taking care of your health becomes exceedingly difficult. It is believed that many empaths have a mental image that they are energy trapped in their body.

Imagine how you would feel if you were not comfortable in your own skin? Your body becomes a prison, one that is too soft, hard, big, small, or tight, trapping all your energies. Even if an empath's body is ideal according to societal standards, it feels terribly wrong. There have been instances when highly sensitive individuals and empaths developed bulimia nervosa because they felt light and close to the true energy source when they were incredibly thin.

General Fatigue and Tiredness

Stress can worsen any physical health issues you already experience. Empaths often feel fatigued after a regular day at work. Even simple tasks such as going to work, spending time with others, or going out for a meal can become exhausting. When you are constantly bombarded by stress from all directions and the activities you indulge in, living life becomes difficult. This overall sense of exhaustion does not leave much time or energy for self-care.

Another common problem that empaths suffer from is guilt. Guilt can induce a lot of stress when left unchecked. Empaths prioritize the wellbeing of others over themselves. After all, they feel what others feel, and if others are happy, they will be happier too. This might sound like a good idea, but all it does is worsen the stress you experience. The daily exhaustion leaves them no energy to even think about their own physical health or happiness. How can you even entertain the idea of going to the gym or running when you have no energy left? This general exhaustion can result in weight gain.

Overcome Overeating and Addictions

Binging on unhealthy foods gives you an easy way out. It gives a feeling of comfort and satisfaction. After going through the reasons discussed in the previous section, it becomes obvious why empaths are susceptible to food addictions and overeating. A common reason why diets fail highly sensitive individuals like empaths is that they are not usually aware of the reasons why they eat. They are unaware of the factors that can trigger food addictions and overeating. To determine if you have an unhealthy relationship with food, here are a few questions you should answer:

- Do you tend to overeat whenever you feel overwhelmed?

- Do carbs, sugar, and all sorts of processed junk foods soothe any discomfort you experience?

- Do you experience any mood swings or mental fatigue when you consume junk food?

- Are you extremely sensitive to the effects of food?

- Do you have any food allergies or intolerances toward common ingredients such as soy, dairy, or gluten?

- Do you feel energetic and happy when you consume healthy and wholesome meals?

- Are you more prone to feeling stressed out when you are thin?

Take the time to answer these questions honestly. You don't have to worry, even if your answer is "yes" to most of them. Your answers will give you a better insight into your unhealthy eating patterns. Once you are aware of your triggers, dealing with the problem without resorting to unhealthy coping mechanisms becomes easier.

Now, take a look at simple tips you can use to replace the unhealthy eating patterns with healthier ones.

Water is quintessential for your overall health and wellbeing. It is recommended that you need to drink at least eight glasses of water daily. This calorie-free beverage not only quenches your thirst but also helps your body expel toxins. In a way, water purifies you from the inside. Whenever you are exposed to negative energies or feel stressed and overwhelmed, drink filtered water. Water also has a purification effect when used externally. Bathing can soothe your body and mind and wash away any impurities, so do not hesitate to bathe whenever you feel overcome by your daily life stresses.

Instead of resorting to food for comfort, learn to deal with your anxiety. Start paying attention to how you feel when you eat certain foods. Make a mental note of the types of foods you lean toward when overwhelmed or experiencing internal turmoil. It gives you a better understanding of your eating patterns. Once you identify any harmful or unhealthy eating patterns, replacing them with positive ones becomes easier.

Whenever you feel stressed, take a break from whatever you are doing and concentrate on your breathing. Visualize that you are breathing in positive energy and expelling negativity. Your breath is incredibly purifying and helps eliminate toxicity.

It is believed that protein can help stabilize an empath's energy and has a grounding effect on them, so increase your intake of protein. You don't have to look for an animal-based protein source, because many vegetarian options are easily available. Make sure that you consume protein with every meal, and it will help restore your energy balance.

Increase your intake of wholesome vegetables and fruit. If you tend to overeat or gain weight easily, pay attention to the foods you consume. Replace unhealthy carbs with healthy carbs present in vegetables and fruit. These ingredients are also rich in several vitamins and nutrients that your body needs to function effectively. Once you take care of your physical health, your mental health will automatically improve. When you are physically fit and active, dealing with anxiety becomes easier. When you fill yourself up with healthy foods, the chances of overeating or binging on unhealthy junk food reduces.

If you are traveling or will be surrounded by others, make sure you are not hungry. Don't allow your blood sugar levels to drop. Low blood sugar increases your susceptibility to external emotions and feelings. It can also affect your mood, so consume at least three meals daily and never skip them.

Food is a source of energy, and if you do not pay attention to it, it results in energy depletion. Develop healthy dietary habits that reduce your sensitivities instead of worsening them.

Observe the Food's Energy

Empaths are sensitive to energy, and this includes food's energy. Does this sound absurd to you? Well, here is a simple example of putting things in perspective. Think of a scenario where you cooked a meal while feeling extremely stressed or agitated. The food you cook absorbs the energy you give out. So, when you consume a meal that has absorbed unnecessary negative emotions, chances are you feel worse than before. Learn to be mindful of your emotions while cooking. Everything in the world is made of energy. This energy is constantly interacting and changing, but it cannot be destroyed.

Certain empaths are extremely sensitive to the pain and suffering of animals. Yes, all empaths are sensitive, but many are more sensitive than others. If such empaths consume any animal-based foods, they might experience and internalize the animal's suffering. This will certainly take away the pleasure of eating and turn the meal into a troubling experience. If you ever feel like this, opt for a plant-based diet. Load up on fresh vegetables and fruit, nuts and seeds, and whole grains.

Since food has energy in it, the energy vibrations of different ingredients vary. In the previous point, it was mentioned that the negative energies absorbed into animal products—because of the torture and toxicity they endured in their life—could be transferred to you when you consume them. Similarly, organic produce increases your sense of feeling grounded. For instance, consuming organic fruit and vegetables makes you feel more grounded and centered. It also enhances your physical health and wellbeing. Organic foods or plant-based foods have higher vibrant energy as opposed to animal-based ones. Try to opt for low-gluten foods and do not contain or have very low levels of refined sugars. Consume more raw foods than cooked to increase your body's positive energy.

Learn to be more grateful for the food you consume. Once you express your gratitude, it increases positive feelings associated with it. Be grateful for all the effort that went into cooking the meal. Also, don't forget to express your gratitude to all those who made this food available to you. Genuine appreciation is an incredibly powerful tool that increases your energy vibrations while sending positive energy into the universe. You receive what you give out, so be mindful of the energy you give away. It also helps form a stronger bond with the food you consume and improves your energy levels.

It is not just the energy present in foods you should be mindful of, but also concentrate on your body's energy for digestion. Did you know certain foods take longer for digestion and take up much of your energy? It is believed that animal meats, especially red meats, are incredibly difficult to digest. Vegetables and fruit can be digested within an hour, while meat and other animal-based foods can take several hours. During this period, your body uses its internal reserves of energy to aid in digesting and absorbing the food you consume. As an empath, maintaining your internal energy levels is important. Dealing with life is draining, and if your body uses more of the energy available to digest the food you eat, you will be left feeling exhausted. So, opt for easily digestible foods and dense in nutrients to enhance your body's energy levels.

Whenever you are cooking, make sure that you are in a good mood. Stay present in the moment and forget about everything else. Learn to cook from your heart, and the food not only tastes better, but it becomes more nourishing. Learning to stay in the present and being mindful is also important for your spiritual and emotional growth. It helps bring peace and calm to you and your general environment.

Practice mindfulness by learning to savor and eat your food slowly. Do not be in a rush, and don't gulp it down in one go. Instead, take the time and concentrate on the meal you consume. While eating, get rid of all distractions to increase your mindfulness. Savor and relish all the different flavors and textures of the food you consume. Chew it slowly and help your body absorb it better.

As mentioned, opt for more plant-based foods, such as legumes, whole grains, raw vegetables, fresh fruit, nuts, and seeds. Start limiting or eliminating dairy products, animal meats, gluten, refined sugars, caffeine, and liquor from your diet. Alcohol and caffeine are neural stimulants. Contrary to popular belief, they don't enhance your mood but act as natural depressants. Once you ride out the high of the stimulant, the low that follows is quite troubling. As an empath, you are more sensitive to these energy changes than others. Eliminating alcohol and caffeine from your diet is a great way to improve your overall health. It also enhances the quality of sleep you get at night. Apart from these two stimulants, another one you should not depend on is nicotine.

There is no such thing as a perfect diet that will fit everyone. The key is to experiment until you feel better about yourself. Pay attention to how your body feels when you consume specific foods. Maintain a food diary to note down all your observations. Do it for a few weeks, and you will get the hang of it. Once you examine your observations, you will realize certain foods improve your energy levels while others deplete them. Start including more of the foods that help your energy while eliminating the ones that deplete them. By eliminating foods that trigger inflammation, such as gluten, dairy, and fried foods, from your diet, you will see a positive change in your physical health and wellbeing. It also reduces your food sensitivities and any digestive issues. There is much to gain from clean eating—from better digestion to clearer skin and enhanced energy levels.

While making any dietary changes, be patient with yourself. Your body will need time to get used to it. Once it does, you will see a positive change in yourself. Also, do not let others discourage you. Prioritizing your wellbeing isn't selfish, and don't let anyone tell you otherwise.

Chapter 5: How Environment Affects an Empath

Surroundings can affect your mood, energy levels, and overall behavior. How do you feel around your loved ones? How do you feel in a crowded room? How do you feel when your surroundings are messy and cluttered? In different situations, you will feel and experience different things, so unsurprisingly, all you surround yourself with can dramatically affect your overall sense of wellbeing. Unless you are perfectly comfortable in your environment, you cannot thrive. In this chapter, you will learn about how your surroundings affect your empathy, an empath's love for nature, the effect of nature on empaths, and creating optimal work and home environments.

Effect of Surroundings on Empaths

Everyone is affected by their surroundings, but it matters more for empaths and highly sensitive individuals. Their high sensitivity to energy can act as an emotional trigger that unleashes a cascade of stress and emotional overload symptoms. This section looks at how simple aspects of one's surroundings can affect an empath.

Clutter

Clutter is mentally draining and exhausting. When you are inundated by clutter, it becomes difficult to think clearly and rationally. It also increases feelings of mental fatigue and causes mood swings. For instance, how do you feel when you are surrounded by junk? It is hard to feel comfortable or at home when surrounded by things you do not need. Eliminating physical clutter is a great way to eliminate mental clutter from your life. This is perhaps one reason why people can concentrate better when they are in clean and organized spaces. If your work desk is filled with objects you don't need, files you are not using, and other junk, how can you think clearly?

A cluttered environment can also make you feel unmotivated and uninterested. A clean and tidy environment promotes growth and keeps you motivated. Most people avoid any difficult tasks or problems because they don't like to feel overwhelmed. This is a basic human trait that enables one to always opt for a path of least resistance. If your surroundings are disorganized and filled with junk, concentrating on important tasks also becomes difficult. For instance, if you are working on a specific task, but your workspace is cluttered with all previous case files or reminders of other tasks, your mind is constantly distracted. Suppose you cannot concentrate on the task at hand, mental stress and worry increase. This, in turn, prevents you from completing the required tasks and increases the burden.

Crowded Spaces

Crowded spaces are incredibly tiring for an empath. When people constantly surround you, you are subconsciously absorbing their energies, emotions, and feelings. As an empath, you tend to feel these things as if they are yours. You might even experience them in your body. When you are surrounded by people all the time, and it becomes difficult to break free of this constant energy exchange, it can quickly overwhelm and tire you. It also increases the stress you experience. An empath needs alone time to recover after spending a lot of time in crowded spaces.

Shared Living Space

Shared living space is not an ideal condition for empaths. Since they desire solitude, shared space can become a hindrance. When it comes to an ideal home or work environment, an empath needs personal space physically and mentally. You need an area to decompress and enjoy time away from others. The absence of a safe haven can take a toll on an empath's overall sense of wellbeing.

An Empath's Love for Nature

An empath's need for alone time to decompress and for self-care is greater than others. Living in a constant state of feeling overwhelmed is tiring and exhausting—physically, mentally, and emotionally. Since this is the norm for empaths, they need a break from it all. The simplest solution to this problem is to spend time in nature. Here are the different ways of how nature helps empaths.

Resets your Body and Mind

Basking in the beauty of nature and soaking up all its glory and warmth helps distract your mind from all the issues and problems you are exposed to. It allows you to break free of everyone else's emotional baggage. You receive the time and space required to process and understand *your* emotions and feelings. In a way, spending time outdoors helps reset your body and mind. It is also an incredible means for self-introspection. Since an empath cannot turn off their sensitivity, taking a break from the source of stimulation is a great idea. The simplest way to do this is to get away from the hustle-bustle of daily city life and head outdoors.

When others constantly surround you, it becomes difficult to understand whose emotions you might be feeling. By retreating into nature, you finally get a chance to listen to your thoughts, feelings, and emotions. When you let go of negativity in nature, more space is created to accommodate positivity.

Healing Power

Exercising in nature has a healing effect on not just empaths but anyone. When you exercise, your body eliminates toxins and creates room for more positive energy. However, if you exercise in the gym or are surrounded by people while exercising, you absorb more negative energy. It is quite similar to going on a juice cleanse to flush out toxins and binging on alcohol. When you exercise in nature or outdoors, there are no toxins or pollutants. All that is left for your body to absorb is the goodness present around you.

Grounding Effect

The element of Earth is associated with a grounding effect. Spending time outdoors and in close connection with the Earth has positive effects on your overall wellbeing. All human beings are made of atoms. Every single cell in the body consists of atoms. Atoms are filled with positive and negative charged particles known as protons and electrons. Atoms tend to lose their electrons when exposed to prolonged periods of stress, inflammation, trauma, or even a toxic environment. These electrons turn into free radicals that trigger inflammation and cause unpleasant health conditions. The straightforward way to counteract and neutralize the harmful effects of these free radicals is through antioxidants. Did you know that the Earth's electromagnetic field is an antioxidant? When you spend time in contact with Earth's healing energy, its positivity is absorbed into your body. It eliminates the stress caused by free radicals and helps soothe your system on a cellular level. The simple act of walking barefoot on the ground or sitting and meditating under a tree's shade can have a soothing effect on your body and mind.

Soothing and Calming

Listening to the rustling of leaves, the pitter-patter of raindrops, the sound of waves, birdsong, and crackling fires are quite soothing. Most people use these sounds of nature to fall asleep or meditate. Why? Because they are gentle and calming instead of the jarring noises of daily life. Living in a city means all your senses are constantly stimulated, whether they are sound, sight, or smells. Living life in a state of hyper-sensory arousal is tiring and extremely stressful. Over a period, you can successfully learn to tune out the external noises, but it does not mean that these noises don't stimulate your senses. As an empath, your hypersensitivity makes it difficult to find the soothing environment you desire in a crowded city. So, spending time in nature, such as sitting by a lake, river, or the ocean, or camping in the forest, can calm you.

Replenishes your Energy

All empaths are naturally wired to helping others. Their giving nature means that they keep giving, giving, and then give more. They do this not because they want to, but it is how they are biologically wired and programmed. In an empath's attempt to make the world a better place, they deplete their personal energy resources. Doing this constantly will push you to breaking point. Whether it's your friends, loved ones, or volunteering at a charity, there is only so much you can give. Once you reach your breaking point, it's quintessential to replenish your energy to function optimally. After all, what good can you be to others if you cannot help yourself?

Placing yourself first is not a sign of selfishness. For an empath, doing this can trigger the onslaught of a guilty conscience. You do not constantly have to work to serve others. Spending time in nature almost feels as if the universe has permitted you to be yourself. It gives you a chance to focus on yourself and your energies instead of others. You can recharge yourself without guilt while doing something you enjoy.

A Break from the Modern World

The hustle-bustle of a frantic and demanding world is truly exhausting. Unsurprisingly, empaths crave a simple life that does not overwhelm their senses. People are frequently assaulted by social media notifications on different electronic devices and other distractions. The constant overload on the senses is draining. Perhaps the simplest break an empath can get from the modern world is to retreat into nature. Even spending thirty minutes out in nature can rejuvenate an empath's energy. Soaking up the sunshine, listening to nature's sounds, and spending time surrounded by beauty sounds more appealing to an empath than staying indoors chained to various gadgets.

After going through this list, you might have finally understood your love and affinity for nature. Nature not only heals; it strengthens and energizes you. It helps eliminate any unnecessary traces of energy and replenishes you with all things positive and desirable.

The Effect of a Full Moon

Nature allows an empath to feel at peace. Natural phenomena such as a full moon or even natural disasters affect empaths. A full moon is believed to be incredibly powerful. It is not just mythology and folklore that supports this claim, but even science backs it up. For instance, in ancient Greece, it was believed the full moon was the goddess Artemis, and in ancient Egypt, she was embodied as the lioness goddess Bastet. In Hawaii, a full moon is known as the goddess Mahina, and pagans believe the moon is responsible for taking care of the passage of time and the different circles of nature. Now, before you write it off as myths or mythology, look at what modern science has to say about this. Science has proven that ocean tides are ruled by Earth's satellite—the moon.

This constant ebb and flow of natural cycles affect the human body and emotions. You might not have realized it, but everyone is sensitive to natural cycles. As an empath, you are more sensitive to this than you probably ever thought. The moon affects the natural cycle of water. About 70 percent of the world is made of water, as is the human body. Water is associated with feelings, emotions, and is a source of intuition, so empaths are influenced by different phases of the moon. The most important of all is the full moon. When the moon is at its brightest, it is the most powerful. A full moon increases your usual sensitivity, intuition and makes you acutely aware of the surrounding energies. This is perhaps the perfect time to practice a self-care ritual. Use the full moon to harness your empathy and strengthen it while shielding yourself from negative energies.

Work with crystals for self-love, such as amethyst, rose quartz, and malachite on a full moon. Find a quiet spot for yourself, preferably outdoors, to absorb the moon's radiant energy. Hold the desired crystal in your hands and meditate. Seek the universe to guide and help you absorb the healing energies given out by these crystals while getting rid of undesirable energies. Certain plants such as Jasmine, cardamom, juniper, and frankincense strengthen your personal energy because they resonate strongly with the moon's energy cycles. Using essential oils derived from these plants can also help. Practicing simple yoga or even going for a light jog at night can help regulate your inner biological clock and promote relaxation and sleep.

The Effect of Natural Disasters

Natural disasters are unfortunate occurrences and often result in loss of human life, resources and leave a trail of destruction in their wake. Whether it is an earthquake, tsunami, or volcanic eruption, natural disasters are difficult, scary, and exhausting. Are you wondering how this is associated with an empath? In the previous section, you were introduced to how nature helps an empath heal and feel a sense of inner peace. When nature is disrupted, an empath's sense of inner peace is also disrupted. Since these individuals are unique and can understand the perspectives and struggles that others go through, they become more sensitive to natural disasters. The victims of a catastrophic event live in a state of fear. "Where will my next meal come from?" "Do we have enough medication?" or "How will we live after this disaster?" become the victims' pressing concerns. As an empath, chances are you might have felt these emotions too. Maybe you even experienced them as if they were yours?

Whether you live in an area affected by a natural disaster or not, your heart goes out to the victims. An activity as simple as watching the news or reading about it in the papers can be problematic to empaths. It becomes a source of intense stress. As an empath, you will want to help them in any way you can. After all, it is your inherent tendency to relieve someone's suffering. Everyone tends to feel helpless when stuck in situations they cannot fix or have little control over. This increases the feeling of discontent and makes you feel totally out of control. All these intense feelings are severely amplified for empaths. Empaths thrive when others around them are happy. If the world is filled with misery, empaths cannot be happy or at peace. So, the next time you feel uncomfortable or experience discomfort within your body that you cannot explain while reading about natural disasters, it is all due to your empathy.

Creating an Optimal Work Environment

A usual workday lasts for about eight hours. You will probably spend about one-third of your life at work. So, it is quintessential to make sure your work environment is optimal. A toxic work environment can quickly drain your energy and reduce your overall productivity. The simplest way to make sure there is no emotional overload on your empathy is to be sure your workspace protects this energy. The three aspects you need to concentrate on when it comes to your work environment are the meaning you derive from your job, the energy of the physical space, and the energy of those who surround you.

You need healthy, energetic boundaries at your workspace. Working in an open or a chaotic office will drain your energy and overwhelm your senses. The simplest way to do this is by placing photographs of your loved ones, family pet(s), or any landscapes that calm you on your desk. Create a small psychological barrier between you and the rest of the world. Protective and healing items such as sacred beads, crystals, or even a small Buddha statue can create an energetic boundary. Whenever possible, walk away from the work environment and head outdoors. Whether it is a ten-minute coffee break or a lunch break, go to a nearby park or step out of the office building, and you will feel better. Perhaps you can use noise-canceling headphones to play soothing music while at work. Drowning out the external noises and sounds really helps.

You can consider purifying the energy at your workspace. You can spritz a little rose water around the desk or room, burn sage if possible, or even light an incense stick. When it comes to burning sage and lighting incense, make sure that it doesn't activate the smoke alarms or disturb other coworkers. Alternatively, you can diffuse essential oils around your desk without disturbing others. Before you start working, meditate at your desk and ask the universe to guide the way. Seek the protective and healing energies it offers and use it to replenish your energies.

Dealing with others, especially energy vampires who drain your energy, is incredibly important. Negative people emit negative energy. As an empath, you are sensitive to this energy, and it is further amplified when absorbed, so setting boundaries and establishing them is a great way to keep toxic people away. Office politics, petty conflicts, feuds, or backbiting can be incredibly draining on your emotional and mental health. If you notice any toxic individuals in your environment, try to maintain a distance from them. If maintaining physical distance is not possible, create a mental barrier. Become conscious of their energies and keep them away. Try to limit your interactions and, if possible, get away from them. Come up with effective strategies to deal with work stress. A simple way to create work-life balance is by not carrying your work stress home. As soon as the work hours end, it is time to let go of your worries and head home. Take time to energize and recuperate. Create and implement a healthy boundary between your work and professional lives.

Creating an Ideal Home Environment

You might have heard the popular saying that the home is where the heart is. Your highly-attuned senses as an empath mean you constantly absorb energies and emotions from others. You view the world using your intuition, feelings, and ability to understand others' feelings. These sensitivities are brilliant gifts, but they can also throw you off balance in your life. Since you are extremely sensitive to your surroundings, they affect you in one way or another, so you must create the ideal home environment, which helps you thrive and flourish as an empath. If you are constantly overwhelmed, agitated, or restless for no apparent reason, it means you're not in the right environment. Living in a dark, dingy, or disorganized home can quickly overwhelm your senses and drain you of whatever little energy you have left. Your home needs to be a place where you can recover and recoup your energies after a tiring day. Your home offers a break from the overwhelming world you live in. This next section looks at simple tips you can use to create the ideal environment at home.

As mentioned earlier, empaths have a deep connection with nature and thrive on it. The simplest way to bring an element of nature to your home is through plants. Surround your space with bright green plants, and it will instantly uplift your spirits. Plants also add a little life and vigor to your surroundings. If not plants, consider placing fresh flowers in the house. Every couple of days, get fresh flowers for your home and add life to it.

An important trait of an empath is their creativity. Your imagination and creativity are your superpowers. When you are surrounded by beauty, you feel inspired and extremely creative. Pursuing beauty is not frivolous, and it certainly is not a sign of vanity. Place colorful paintings or other artwork, crystals, photographs, memorabilia, and other knick-knacks in your surroundings to enhance your creativity and imagination. When you are surrounded by beauty and color, you instantly feel better about yourself.

Make sure that the colors in your home are uplifting. Instead of opting for exceptionally bright or dark colors that dim your energy, opt for pleasant and pleasing shades. Pastel hues and neutral colors work well instead of dark colors such as red, black, gray, or dark blue. It is not just the colors you should pay attention to but also the lighting. Allow natural light to flood your home, and if not, there should be enough artificial lighting to compensate for it. Avoid dull lighting and opt for bright and pleasant lights.

The colors also influence your levels of motivation, stress, energy, and overall mood. For instance, a bright red color suggests aggression, while yellow can induce anxiety. Stress can also be triggered if you live in a cluttered home. Spend time and start decluttering. If you watched the Netflix series *Tidying Up with Mary Kondo*, you probably realize the importance of decluttering your living space. Surrounded by clutter or unnecessary junk can quickly tire you out. Go through all your possessions and hold on to only those items that add value or meaning to your life. If an item does not fulfill either of these conditions, discard it. Decluttering is also a stress buster and mood enhancer. Use the basic principle of decluttering in all aspects of your life.

As an empath, you need time away from others, so you need a space where no one else is allowed, and that truly belongs to you. It does not have to be a big room. Even a small corner of the house can be your Zen den. Meditate in this spot, get away from the stresses of daily life, and use it for self-introspection. If others live in the house, make sure that you get space for yourself, and no one else intrudes on your alone time.

Empaths are incredibly sensitive to strong aromas and chemicals. If you want to leave your home smelling pleasant and soothing while calming your mind without polluting the air, use essential oils. Essential oil diffusers will come in handy. Diffusing lavender, orange, bergamot, or ylang-ylang essential oils at home will create a comforting environment.

By following the simple tips discussed in this section, you can instantly elevate your mood and eliminate any negative energy. You cannot control many things in life, but you can certainly regulate your environment to suit your needs and desires. Don't hesitate to take the necessary action to enhance your empathy and reduce the chances of getting overwhelmed. When your environment is conducive to growth, love, and development, it instantly makes you feel better. When you feel better about yourself, your quality of life improves.

Chapter 6: The Importance of Balanced Living

Math teaches that every function needs to be balanced. The same logic applies to your life. If you want to lead a happy and healthy life, there needs to be balance. If you feel like you have little or no control over your life, it means your life lacks balance. A common mistake many people make when it comes to happiness is the belief it stems from external sources. People associate happiness with different things in life. For instance, you might tell yourself you will be happy when you buy your dream home, get your ideal job, or something else along these lines.

Remember, all these things are goals, but they are not the means to happiness. True happiness stems from within and cannot be taken away. No one can take your joy away unless you let them. Happiness often lies in little things in life. Are you wondering what the relationship between happiness and balance is? One cannot exist without the other. You cannot be happy if your life is unbalanced, and the lack of balance makes you unhappy. Leading a balanced life is a fine art. What might work for others does not necessarily have to work for you. Your idea of balance can be quite different from what others believe or perceive it to be.

In this chapter, you will learn about balancing different aspects of your life as an empath.

Different Aspects of Life

So, what does it mean to live a balanced life? It essentially means that different elements in your life do not overwhelm one another, and you control them. It also means there is no discord between your heart and mind. Imagine how difficult life would become if your heart went in one direction while your mind tells you to do something else? When you live a well-balanced life, your heart and mind work in synergy and help you move in the right direction without internal turmoil or power struggle. A well-balanced life makes you feel motivated, grounded, calm, happy and focused.

Now, you might be wondering how you can live a balanced life. The answer is quite simple. The first thing you need to do is concentrate on different aspects of your life. Every element in your life can be broadly classified into two categories: internal and external. Imbalances in life occur when you focus more on one aspect and forget about the other. There needs to be harmony between your life's internal and external components to feel balanced and at peace.

For instance, when you solely focus on your life's external aspects, such as relationships, work, or activities, it doesn't leave much time, energy, or strength to deal with your internal self. By focusing on these external aspects, you are avoiding what is going on within your body, mind, heart, and soul. On the other hand, if you spend all your time on self-reflection, you forget about the life that goes on around you.

Three things fall under your life's internal components: heart, mind, and health. You need to challenge your mind intellectually, create opportunities to thrive and grow, and give it the rest it requires. When it comes to your heart, you need to strike a balance between giving and receiving love. It can never be a one-way street. As an empath, chances are you are inclined toward being the giver in every situation in life. The problem this poses is that you end up with little or no love for yourself. Dear empath, you will be tempted to help everyone who comes your way because you are naturally giving. But it would be best if you directed your empathy and compassion toward yourself too.

You need and deserve empathy as much as those around you. The different components of your inner life that you need to concentrate on are your physical and mental health. You need to maintain a healthy diet, exercise regularly, and get enough rest. Similarly, it would help if you also struck a balance between doing all these things and treating yourself occasionally. When you deprive yourself of one thing because you are solely focused on another, it creates much imbalance. You might not realize its effect immediately, but eventually, it all catches up and becomes a big problem.

Now, concentrate on the external aspects of your life. There are four areas: social setting, work or career, family, and fun. When it comes to working, you need to set certain goals to excel in life and move ahead. While you do this, try to see the bigger picture and enjoy the journey you are on. If you concentrate solely on your goals, you forget about the journey—the life you are living.

Look at the social component of your life. It would help if you took time for yourself as an empath, but it does not mean isolation. Self-isolation is not the answer. Similarly, you need not become a social butterfly. However, as an empath, you cannot spend all your time socializing because it becomes incredibly draining. Striking a balance between spending time with yourself and others is important for overall wellbeing. All your obligations and relationships, whether they are with your family or romantic relationships, are important. While you do this, do not forget about drawing certain boundaries. As an empath, you are probably used to going out of your way to please and help others. If you don't have any boundaries, you end up compromising things that matter most to you. Allocate enough time to indulge in activities you enjoy. It would help if you struck a balance between doing this and ensuring you don't go overboard while enjoying your life.

By now, it is pretty obvious that life exists on a spectrum. You need to make sure that both ends of the spectrum are well balanced. If you move to an extreme, it throws off your balance.

Realign Your Life

Have you ever seen a tightrope walker? They need to walk on a rope that is suspended above the ground. The goal is to get from one end to the other without losing balance. To maintain balance, a tightrope walker uses a long bar. Well, life is just like this. In the previous section, you were introduced to different aspects of life you should concentrate on. Even if one of these aspects is imbalanced, it affects all the other areas. Life is a balancing act. Empaths need to learn to strike the right balance between their internal and external lives for their health and happiness. This section looks at a few simple and practical tips you can use to attain this objective.

Take Stock and Acknowledge

Before you can rebalance your life, it is important to take stock of where you are at this time. Assess your life and everything else going on. It is okay to acknowledge that certain aspects of your life have no balance. You cannot achieve harmony if you do not accept a certain amount of discord. This acceptance is liberating and empowering. It gives you a better understanding of what you desire in life. Once you have a better understanding of yourself, life gets easier.

Set Goals

You need to set goals in different aspects of your life—set goals for your health, mental wellbeing, social life, and career. Whenever you set certain goals, it gives you a sense of direction and purpose in life. When you know where you are headed, it becomes easier to take the necessary action to get there. Since empaths are constantly overwhelmed by others' emotions and feelings that are not their own, these goals act as homing beacons. It is not just about setting goals; you need to plan and prepare to achieve these goals.

Conscious Decision

Make a conscious decision to rebalance your life. Unless you make this decision and commitment, you cannot move ahead. When you choose reality as the path that guides your decisions, regaining balance becomes easier. Making a conscious decision to change ensures you stick to this rule when it comes to decision-making. This also reduces any stress you experience.

Take Risks

There are no rewards in life if you do not take risks. Assess yourself and be willing to step out of your comfort zone. Taking risks not only presents several opportunities for growth and development, but it enhances your overall life. It makes you more aware of what life is about and your skill set. Don't be afraid to take risks. Instead, acknowledge that without risks, you will never get anywhere in life. Recognize the importance of balance in your life and work to recreate it so that every risk you take is worth it.

Empower Yourself

Learn to empower yourself. There will be instances when life does not go your way, or you are overwhelmed by other things. In such instances, please learn to be kind to yourself. Creating any semblance of balance in life becomes tricky if you are too harsh on yourself. As an empath, you might be used to being compassionate to others. Extend this compassion toward yourself, and things will get better.

Prepare and Plan

Life is unpredictable, but you can reduce this unpredictability by planning and preparation. Whenever you make a plan, you prepare yourself for all the setbacks or obstacles you might face. This is a great way to regain a sense of balance and control over your life. For instance, if you know you have several official and personal commitments in the following week, make a schedule. By doing this, you can make sure that you are fulfilling all your obligations without any compromises. It also gives you better insight into how you spend your time.

Self-introspection

Do not forget to set aside time for self-introspection. No matter what, self-introspection is essential to growth. It also helps you understand the activities to do to make sure your life is balanced. You never really know how well you are doing or the areas you are lagging in until you reassess your position. No decision you make is set in stone. If something is not working for you, change it. You cannot bring about this change without introspection and self-assessment. Before you sleep at night, review the day you had, and look at the positive and negative aspects. If you believe there is scope for improvement, work on it the following day. You can also plan for the next day, so you feel more organized in the morning.

Ideas for a Well-balanced Lifestyle

Here are simple ways to balance different aspects of your life as an empath.

Physical Health

Diet, exercise, sleep, and rest are the four aspects you need to optimize to maintain your physical health. Since empaths are extremely sensitive, they cannot lead a balanced life unless they concentrate on all these aspects. You cannot discount the importance of nutrition when it comes to a balanced diet. Eating healthily promotes your mental functioning and maintains your overall mood. Make sure that you consume a diet rich in vegetables, proteins, and fruit. A healthy and wholesome diet ensures you reach and maintain your ideal weight. Follow the simple diet tips discussed in the previous section, and you will see a positive change in your physical health. Apart from diet, concentrate on exercise, sleep, and the rest you get.

Make it a point to exercise for at least twenty minutes daily. Any exercise is good, and it does not have to be a gym session. Whether it is swimming, running, jogging, or playing a sport, add physical activity to your daily routine. A combination of diet and exercise will improve your overall fitness, strength, and stamina.

Adults need seven-nine hours of good quality sleep at night. Remember, it is not just the duration of sleep that matters; it is also the quality. It doesn't make sense if you sleep for ten hours but keep waking up after every hour or two. Disturbed sleep increases the stress levels and prevents your body from functioning effectively, reducing your cognitive functioning. Sleep deprivation is the leading cause of several chronic illnesses. A simple tip you can use to improve your sleep quality is to create a soothing bedtime ritual.

Taking a calming bath, changing into comfortable clothes, engaging in light reading, or listening to soothing music can be a part of your sleep schedule. Make sure that you wake up and sleep at the same time daily, even on the weekends. It helps regulate your circadian rhythm. The bedroom environment must be conducive to good quality sleep. Avoid harsh lighting, maintain an ideal temperature, and make sure it isn't noisy. Give your body and mind five minutes every day to unwind. You can meditate, do light yoga, or even give yourself a soothing massage to de-stress.

Mental Health

To improve and balance your mental health, it is important to stay on top of all the tasks you need to complete. Dealing with stress is a great way to enhance your mental health, so start your day by setting achievable goals you can work toward. The goals need to be small and not too complicated. At the end of the day, review all the activities you completed and whether you attained the goals or not. Whenever you notice scope for improvement in your life, work on it.

Another great way to keep up your motivation levels is to create a to-do list. Wake up early and make a list of all the tasks you want to accomplish in a day. If you do not have time early in the morning, you can do it before you go to sleep at night. So, as soon as you wake up, you know all the things you need to complete. It helps prioritize your responsibilities and accomplish things that add meaning to your life. This simple activity also reduces unnecessary mental stress and burden. As an empath, you already experience a great deal of stress when exposed to crowds and others' emotions— you don't need any added stress. Make it a point to concentrate on activities that help enhance your life and add meaning. No, it is not about your career; instead, indulge in activities that make you happy. You can read, paint, dance, sing, or do anything else that makes you joyful. Concentrating on your hobbies adds value to your life and reduces stress. Since empaths are naturally creative, indulging in a hobby increases your creativity and imagination.

Spend time and get in touch with your spiritual self. Spirituality and religion are not synonymous. You can be spiritual even if you do not believe in a specific religion. It is entirely up to you and is a personal choice. To engage your spirituality, meditate, do yoga, or walk in nature. Spending time outdoors and connecting with nature helps recharge and reenergize your batteries and prepares you for everything life has in store.

Social Needs

Most empaths lean toward introversion, but excessive isolation is never desirable, and it certainly is not a good thing. When you isolate yourself from everyone else, it increases the risk of depression and anxiety while reducing your self-confidence and self-esteem. Understandably, empaths need a bit of alone time. Learn to strike a balance between the solitude you desire and socializing.

A healthy social life is important for your mental and emotional health. Social life does not mean attending parties or visiting crowded places every night. It can be something as simple as meeting friends for a meal or chatting with them. Catch up on everything that is going on in others' lives and stay involved. Don't isolate yourself as your loved ones are your support system. While you do this, make sure that you set healthy boundaries too. It is okay to help your friends and family, but not at great personal cost and not always. By establishing personal boundaries and implementing them, it helps increase your self-confidence while maintaining healthy relationships. If you let others consume you entirely in the relationship's name, you will be left with nothing at the end of the day.

Work-Life Balance

Establishing work-life balance is a critical aspect of a well-balanced life. Do not compromise on your personal life for the sake of your career and vice versa. If you do this, it breeds contempt and unhappiness. It also increases mental turmoil and emotional stress. While at work, avoid any distractions and concentrate purely on the work. Once you leave the office premises, forget about the work stress and try not to carry it home. Establish and implement clear boundaries when it comes to your work-life relationship.

Do not get overwhelmed by the different tips given in this chapter. They are quite easy to follow and practical. The first thing you need to do is accept that you are the only one who can control your life. Even if a situation seems hopeless, there is always a choice available. Start by implementing these tips one at a time—don't try to do it all at once if you want to succeed. By learning to balance your life, you get a better understanding of yourself and your empathy.

Chapter 7: Pitfalls Empaths Should Avoid

Life as an empath is not always easy. Your superpowers can cause hurdles in life when left unchecked. This section looks at simple pitfalls all empaths must avoid if they want to lead happy, healthy, and successful lives.

Dealing with Anger

Anger is a natural human emotion, and everyone experiences it from time to time. It is also one of the most powerful and potentially destructive emotions. Since all the emotions are amplified for an empath, anger is amplified too. The primary reason for this is that empaths tend to feel things first and react immediately. There is hardly any time for the thought process. This makes anger incredibly potent for empaths. The intensity of an emotion is directly proportional to the connection. The more intense a reaction is, the deeper the connection.

There are two usual responses empaths have when it comes to dealing with anger. The empath will either have an angry outburst, flee, or distance themselves from the situation causing the anger. This is why empaths get extremely overwhelmed and stimulated when exposed to intense emotions and anger. Therefore, if there were instances when you felt extremely angry or maybe even cried out of frustration, it is due to your empathy. Your empathy amplifies the basic anger you feel, and it manifests into something bigger and scarier than it actually is.

Anger is extremely complicated for an empath because they are aware of emotions before others are aware of them. This kind of anger becomes a major hurdle, especially if the person you are angry with is your romantic partner. This can also happen with a coworker. When you let anger cloud your judgment and give in to the intense emotions and reactions, others will withdraw. When others start withdrawing, attacking, or avoiding you or the situation altogether, it further intensifies your anger. This, in turn, also increases any stress you experience.

An angry empath is similar to an angry tiger confined to a cage. All it can do is pace around miserably, waiting to pounce or even escape. Well, none of these reactions are desirable or even practical. Anger is a secondary emotion that is used to mask a primary emotion. As an empath, you not only feel your anger, but you can also experience others' anger. Since everything is magnified, learning to cope with anger is quintessential for your overall wellbeing.

There are different physical forms in which anger can manifest, ranging from headaches to insomnia, depression, and even high blood pressure. The inability to process and control one's anger can worsen physical health. It, in turn, can increase mental stress and further aggravate the anger. Do you realize that the inability to deal with anger is a vicious self-fueling cycle? Unprocessed anger picked up from others is extremely uncomfortable. Any old anger that is still present within you can quickly turn into bitterness or resentment when left unchecked. On the other hand, fresh pain feels like you are standing too close to an open flame and is uncomfortable.

The most common reason why people feel angry is fear. Fear is a primary emotion that triggers the secondary emotion—anger. The next time you feel angry, give yourself a moment to regain composure. Take a step back and try to view the situation from a neutral perspective. When you peel away the first layer of your anger, you will realize it is due to some fear or pain. Anger acts as a shield that protects you from this fear or pain presented with it. Sadly, it does not help resolve the issue and merely worsens the situation.

When you feel angry, the first thing you need to do is question whose anger you feel. If it is your anger, consider the reasons why you might be angry before reacting. Learn to respond instead of reacting. When you respond, it means you are calmly and rationally thinking about the situation instead of allowing your emotions to guide the way. If you realize the anger you are feeling is not even your own, send it away. You have complete control over your emotions, and you do not need to absorb others' unhealthy emotions. Remind yourself of this truth whenever you are overwhelmed by others. As an empath, you are a natural healer and nurturer. Channel your inner compassion and let it guide the way instead of your anger. Since you can think from others' perspectives, use this strength to melt away your anger.

Susceptibility to Addictions

In one of the previous chapters, you were introduced to the idea of why empaths are susceptible to addictions. Whether it is overeating or dependence on alcohol, drugs, or any other substance, an empath's susceptibility to addictions cannot be overlooked. The main reason they depend on other substances or unhealthy coping mechanisms is that they cannot deal with their emotions. The constant emotional stimulation coupled with the highly challenging world and stressful lives people lead these days can be too much for an empath to bear.

Addiction is not just a mere distraction; it can also disrupt and destroy your life when left unchecked. Empaths are not like normal individuals, and they are certainly not destined to lead a normal life. Empathy, which sets them apart from others, can also become a weakness. The inability to deal with painful emotions or not understanding the source of these emotions and lack of self-awareness can trigger loneliness. In a bid to cope with all these things, empaths get misdirected in the process. The inability to effectively and efficiently understand and process all the energy an empath keeps interacting with can take a toll on one's physical, emotional, and mental health. Any toxic accumulation of low vibrating energies stored within an empath's body can quickly drain their personal energy.

If you do not want to get stuck in the never-ending vicious cycle of dependence and addiction, it is important to understand yourself and the gift of empathy. The simplest way to enhance your overall productivity and cope with all the feelings, sensations, and energies you experience is to get sufficient rest. Take a break from your routine, disconnect from the world, and concentrate on yourself.

Everyone is quite hard on themselves, especially empaths. No human being is perfect. People have flaws and emotional baggage to deal with, and empaths are no different. To manage life as an empath, it is important to accept yourself the way you are. Don't allow any emotional buildup and listen to your body's signals. Let go of any resistance, and don't hold on to emotions or feelings that hurt you. Whether it is a traumatic event, an unpleasant experience, or a major lifestyle change, let it go regardless of the situation or the circumstances—and don't carry the disagreeable emotions. Also, spend some time understanding your emotions and separating them from the ones you pick up from others. Start managing your energy, time, and emotions. Learn to set certain personal boundaries and implement them.

People Pleasing

Empaths love to please others. Since they experience and feel what others feel, they try to make everyone comfortable and happy. In an attempt to do this, they end up ignoring themselves. As an empath, you need to stop trying to please everyone. The simple truth of life is you cannot please everyone, and the only person you can is yourself. When you try to make people happy, you end up disappointing yourself. Stop seeking external approval, validation, or happiness. Your true source of happiness stems from within.

People-pleasing can increase mental stress and even hurt your self-esteem and self-confidence. Do not be under any misconceptions that people-pleasing is the same as generosity. Your empathy lets you be generous and helpful to others. Generosity stems from a healthy self-regard and a sense of genuine happiness you derive in a shared environment. On the other hand, people-pleasing often comes from a place that requires someone else's approval. When you try to please others, you are making yourself subservient to their needs and desires. In this process, you will have no time, energy, or resources to concentrate on your life in general. If others' opinions matter more than yours, you cannot get anywhere in life.

Therefore, it is ideal to concentrate on yourself before anyone else. As an empath, you might feel a little guilty while prioritizing yourself. This is a sign of self-respect, self-esteem, and self-confidence. It shows you have a healthy personality and are not hesitant to implement these aspects. It reduces any chances of others taking you for granted. It also gives you better control and understanding of yourself and life in general. Learn to say "no" and stand up for yourself. If you don't do this, no one else can do it for you. Being assertive and setting boundaries means protecting yourself. This is not selfish, but it is a great way to reduce others' expectations, judgments, and unnecessary responsibilities. It finally gives you a chance to accept the truth that you have no control over other people's lives or emotions. You are not responsible for how they feel, and you are certainly not accountable for their actions. Practice the simple skill of saying no.

Emotional Sponges

An undeniable truth about empaths is that they are emotional sponges. Empaths are openhearted individuals who trust their intermission and are not scared to wear their hearts on their sleeves. The openheartedness of an empath can never be taken away from them. Conversation with an empath can help even the most unlikely person to open up. However, such experiences can be quite harrowing and exhausting for an empath without boundaries. Since empaths struggle to maintain and implement personal boundaries, they become emotional sponges who constantly soak up everything in their environment. It can be the emotions, feelings, or even physical symptoms of pain that they absorb from others. When left unchecked, it increases the emotional baggage an empath feels. Empaths certainly have immense power within, but the dark side of this ability is that they often forget about themselves.

What happens when you place a sponge in a bowl of water? After a few seconds, the sponge will soak up all the water. The sponge becomes heavy and dense because of it. This is precisely what happens to an empath's energy when they constantly pick up energies from others. Unfortunately, most of the emotional turmoil empaths experience is not the result of their emotions; it's the combined turmoil of the collective emotions around them. If left unchecked, this kind of emotional baggage can quickly turn into a mental health condition. From anxiety to depression, empaths are susceptible to developing mental health disorders. Grounding and shielding yourself is a great way to protect your personal energy while helping others. Another technique is to set boundaries in all aspects of your life. You will learn more about shielding and enhancing your empathy in the subsequent chapters.

Energy Vampires

Energy vampires and other toxic personalities, such as narcissists, are attracted to empaths. Likewise, empaths are attracted to them like moths to a flame. Energy vampires and narcissists are usually devoid of empathy. Energy vampires know empaths are a source of heightened energy and resources that they need to survive. An empath can understand someone else's perspective and is good at offering compassion and empathy whenever required. Empaths do not hesitate to give people the benefit of the doubt and give several chances to prove themselves. All the emotional labor that an empath offers seems quite attractive to narcissists and other emotional vampires.

Energy vampires and toxic individuals are in dire need of healing. This healing cannot come from an external source, and it needs to be an internal process based on self-reflection and growth. However, these individuals are not usually inclined to do this and believe that an empath's energy will help them achieve a level of healing they require without any effort. A narcissist and other energy vampires abuse an empath's compassion. They can pretty much get away with any toxic behavior without any accountability.

An empath's willingness to adapt to the situation is exploited and misused. In the end, empaths tend to get stuck in toxic or downright abusive relationships with the energy vampire. Because empaths are naturally giving while toxic individuals are always taking, the equation is always imbalanced. In such relationships, the empath keeps giving and does not receive anything in return. The appetite of an emotional vampire is perfectly satiated when they devour an empath's energy.

As an empath, you need to realize you are not responsible for anyone else's behavior. You can be compassionate to others but understand that not everyone deserves it. Start caring for yourself and allow others to care for you. In a healthy and happy relationship, there is always reciprocity.

Loss of Identity

Losing your identity or understanding of oneself is quite painful and shattering. If you cannot identify or understand yourself, how can you understand life or others around you? Since empaths spend all their time and energy catering to others' needs, they have little or no time left for themselves. When others' emotions and feelings constantly bombard them, they have time to process their emotions and feelings. After a while, an empath can reach a point where they cannot distinguish their emotions from others. In fact, chances are they will start questioning their feelings. It becomes difficult to understand where they end and others begin. If all this sounds familiar to you, it can be a sign of an identity crisis. The simplest way to understand yourself is by spending more time on self-reflection. Concentrate on healing yourself before you help others.

Chapter 8: Empaths and Relationships

As an empath, you have a keen sense of awareness and extreme sensitivity to others' emotions and feelings. This is a brilliant gift in any relationship. After all, imagine all the misunderstandings that could be reduced if you could view things from someone else's perspective. There are several benefits of empathy, but it does come with challenges too. In this section, you will learn about the best personality types suitable for an empath, secrets to loving an empath, and tips to maintain healthy and happy relationships with empaths.

As mentioned in the previous chapter, empaths are like magnets for toxic individuals and energy vampires. Therefore, you must not fall prey to an energy vampires' manipulative ways. It does not mean you must never be on guard. Instead, it means to pay attention to your intuition when it comes to a romantic partner. If your gut says something is wrong, trust it.

Energy vampires and toxic individuals can seem quite charming. In fact, if they turn up the charm, you will be easily disarmed. It is time to understand that this is how they function and use their charm to get their way. Once the energy vampire has your attention, they will slowly work their way into your life. For a sensitive empath, this is a recipe for disaster. Therefore, it's important to pay attention to the people you let into your life. If your partner makes you feel guilty or remorseful about things you have not done, it's a sign of a toxic relationship.

Another red flag you must not ignore is the lack of reciprocity. If you give, your partner needs to reciprocate. If it feels like your partner has taken you for granted, chances are they have. If your partner cannot respect your boundaries, it is also a sign of a toxic relationship. If you feel you are in a relationship with an individual who has little or no regard for your feelings and the entire relationship is about them, break free of it. The sooner you let go of toxic relationships, the easier it is to move forward. Remember the rule about decluttering mentioned in the previous chapter? Well, time to use that rule and start decluttering your personal life and relationships. If a relationship does not add any value to your life and drains your energy, you don't need it.

Truth About Empaths and Relationships

An empath experiences life that no one else can begin to imagine. Whether it is happiness, sadness, or any other emotion, everything is magnified for an empath. It's human nature to try to change things that are not appealing. However, this cannot be done for an empath in a relationship. No one can change the way an empath views life. Empaths are rare, and they need to be cherished. As an empath, if you try to change yourself to please others, it increases your dissatisfaction in the relationship and will drain you quickly. Empaths need to be understood the way they are. If you do not want to alienate yourself, don't try to change. It is highly unlikely that you will not experience emotions or feelings deeply. However, you can talk about these things with your partner. Don't shut yourself off; learn to be open and honest with your partner.

An empath needs time alone. You probably realize the importance and benefits of doing this. You cannot spend all your time with another individual, even if it is your soulmate. You need time for yourself so that you can recuperate. This is not something everyone is capable of understanding, especially in a romantic relationship. It often causes various misunderstandings where an empath's partner might feel left out, disgruntled, or even upset. Therefore, it is important to find someone who not only understands but also respects your needs. Needing time for yourself is not selfish, and it is good for your health and the relationship. If you need to disappear for a while, don't do it randomly. Instead, inform your partner about why you need it and go ahead. It's all about open and honest communication if you want the relationship to survive.

Empaths are extremely creative and imaginative. Therefore, it is highly unlikely that a relationship with an empath will be boring. However, this creativity and imagination do come with a downside. For instance, an empath's ideas might sound outlandish or even unorthodox. It can make others feel uncomfortable and dubious. It, in turn, can cause problems in the relationship. Once an empath sets their mind to something, they will do it. If you struggle with your imagination and creativity as an empath in a relationship, the first thing you need to do is talk to your partner about it. Whenever you have a conversation about it, listen to them with an open heart and mind. If your partner is telling you something, it comes from a place of love and understanding. Also, it gives you another perspective to think about the situation. Use your empathy to get a better understanding of the situation and make an informed decision.

Since empaths are human lie detectors, no one can keep the truth from them. You need a partner who will always be open and honest. Even a white lie can become a major problem for an empath. They can see through others' intentions, motivations, and inclinations. This sense of intuition an empath is blessed with is extremely helpful in life. However, it can make your partner feel controlled in a relationship. If you keep telling them about the things that can go wrong—yes, you are probably right about it—it can worry your partner or even scare them. Also, imagine how you would feel if someone told you what you were supposed to do all the time. In an attempt to help others, empaths can come across as controlling and dominating.

For a healthy and happy relationship, strike a balance between your strengths and weaknesses as an empath. Talk to your partner about all things, and do not shut them out. Certain accommodations need to be made by both parties. However, if you are willing to make this commitment, it will be worth your while.

Tips to Cultivate Healthy Relationships for Empaths

As an empath, you are probably used to living with a variety of intense emotions. In such instances, how can you possibly have time for anyone else if you're struggling to find time for yourself? This is a common question all empaths need to answer when it comes to relationships. This section looks at some simple and practical tips you can use to cultivate healthy and positive relationships.

The first thing you need to do is understand there is a difference between cognitive and emotional empathy. Cognitive and emotional empathy are the two basic types of empathy. Cognitive empathy is the ability to understand someone else's emotions without believing them to be yours. Emotional empathy is when you experience the same emotions the other person feels as if they are yours. In a healthy relationship, there is a place for emotional and cognitive empathy. However, learning to understand and distinguish between these two things is quintessential. Understand this difference, and it will save you from a world of pain and internal turmoil. For instance, if you suddenly feel low or extremely unhappy for no apparent reason, it's time to question if you feel your emotions or are absorbing them from your partner?

Life can be tiring and overwhelming and even more so for empaths. Living as a highly sensitive person in this world is exhausting. Since you are extremely receptive and perceptive of everything going on within and around you, it is emotionally draining. The same is true for your relationship. Even if you love your partner unconditionally, it's important to take some time out for yourself. It helps regroup your thoughts and put things in perspective. There are different ways in which you can recoup after an extremely tiring day. If you need time for yourself, talk to your partner about it. If your partner understands your need for alone time, it is a sign of a healthy relationship, but if he or she doesn't, it can soon turn into a toxic relationship.

When two people start living together, there will be a difference of opinions. Empaths are good listeners, and it is a trait that will help your relationship. That said, you need to understand it is only about listening. Listen carefully to what your partner says, but you do not have to accept it as the truth if you don't believe them. Remember, you don't have to do everything your partner says or feel the way they do if it doesn't feel right. Stand by your values and if anything goes against it, put your foot down. It helps establish healthy boundaries without making your partner feel left out. Accept that you will have different points of view but learn to listen patiently.

Spending time together is as important as spending time apart. You do not need to do everything together and certainly don't have to spend every waking minute together. Learn to do things by yourself and encourage your partner to do the same. Give them the time, space, and opportunity to do this. Grow as individuals and work on growing together as a couple. This is important for any relationship and incredibly important for an empath. If you spend all your time together, you will pick up your partner's energy vibes and emotions. It is unhealthy and will become emotionally tiring. As an empath, your needs might be unique. Don't crowd each other and take the time and space required for yourself.

A difference of opinions between two individuals is common. When this happens, criticism is bound to crop up. Any criticism you receive can be dealt with constructively. That said, allow your intuition to guide the way when your partner asks you to change. If you are in a happy and healthy relationship, your partner will understand your empathy. They will help and support you whenever you need it. Instead, if you are constantly criticized, your efforts are ignored, or you are taken for granted, these are some red flags you must never overlook. Trust your gut when it comes to romantic relationships. If you hear the alarm bells ringing in your head, pay extra attention to them.

Best Personality Types for an Empath

Empaths are highly sensitive individuals, and they need someone who can understand and respect their sensitivity. A happy and healthy relationship is one that is filled with unconditional love and acceptance. In such a relationship, each partner not only supports the other, but there is also mutual love and respect. When this love, respect, adoration, and acceptance exist, it increases the partner's self-confidence and happiness. It also helps strengthen the bond they share. However, a romantic relationship is seldom easy for an empath. As mentioned in the previous section, there are various things an empath needs, and it might not always be easy to find an accommodating partner. An empath craves companionship, but they do not feel safe being truly vulnerable, and learning to navigate the relationship while protecting their sensitivities is important. The first step toward forming a healthy relationship is to find the right partner. Based on your temperament and needs as an empath, your ideal partner or soulmate falls into four different categories.

The Empath

A relationship with an empath is wonderful. If your partner is also an empath, it makes things easier. Such relationships consist of highly sensitive individuals who are aware of each other's emotions and perspectives. It reduces any chances of unnecessary miscommunications and prevents misunderstandings. You are each finely tuned into the emotions of the other and tend to feel everything quite extremely. There is an obvious disadvantage of being in a relationship with an empath—emotions run high. You can both get overwhelmed by each other's feelings.

Two overly sensitive individuals living together will become a recipe for disaster if neither of you knows how to harness and protect your energies. Therefore, before you enter into a relationship with an empath, spend some time understanding your empathy. You not only need to honor your empathy but your partner's too. If the relationship consists of two empaths who are constantly overrun by the world's problems, it will increase the anxiety in the relationship and at home. Therefore, each of you must get some alone time and space to recover. The great news is that you do not have to explain all these things to the other person, because they will understand it immediately. It can be challenging for two empaths to fall in love and maintain a mutually happy and fulfilling relationship. Well, this is possible if there is mutual respect, open communication, and lots of unconditional love and acceptance.

The Thinker

The intellectual or intense thinking personality is a good match for empaths. Those who belong to this personality type are quite bright, can optimally articulate their thoughts, and are comfortable with their thoughts. These individuals view the world through rational logic and thought. Empaths are quickly overwhelmed by emotions and thoughts, whereas thinkers are not. They stay rational even in intense situations and are known to keep their calm. Their calm presence brings a sense of balance to the empath's life. They also have much to learn from their empath counterparts. An empath can teach them to trust their gut, embrace their feelings, and be more lighthearted and sensual. The thinker and the empath make up for each other's shortcomings in the relationships, making the partnership fruitful and fulfilling.

The Gusher

Some individuals are acutely aware of their emotions and are in touch with them. They only experience such emotions powerfully but love to share them with others too. As the name suggests, those who belong to this personality type often gush love and praise. They are adept at quickly processing any negativity and can easily move away from negative experiences and replace them with positivity.

They might constantly overshare and not know where to draw the line in a relationship on the downside. This can soon become tiring for an empath as the gusher's intense and constant need to share all their emotions creates an emotional overload. If an empath and the gusher are to be successful partners, there needs to be a balance between emotional sharing. As an empath in a relationship, you need to set certain boundaries and implement them without compromising. These limits will prevent any emotional overload and will also show the gusher where to draw the line.

The Rock

Rocks are strong and silent personality types. They are stable, dependable, and consistent. These are three characteristics that an empath always looks for in a relationship. These individuals will neither judge nor get upset if you share your emotions. In a way, they create the perfect environment in a relationship for an empath to be their true selves. In a world where empaths help others and are always depended on, individuals with this personality type become an empath's pillar of strength and support. After all, everyone needs people they can rely on in times of need.

Empaths and rocks make extremely good partners. The relationship will be well balanced, where each partner promotes and supports the other's growth and development. The only downside of a relationship with this personality type is that they might not be accustomed to freely expressing their emotions. However, they can certainly learn how to do all this from their empath partners. An empath can learn to stay grounded and centered from their rock counterpart. As mentioned, you each have something to learn from the other.

Chapter 9: The Best Careers for Empaths

Empaths thrive in a low-stress environment. Therefore, it can be challenging to come up with an ideal form of employment for an empath. Traditionally, they tend to excel in small companies, solo jobs, and other low-stress arenas. Working full- or part-time from home is an ideal situation where the emphasis is away from the frenzy of office politics, toxic coworkers, and constant interaction with others. A job where you can plan your schedule and breaks according to your needs and requirements is ideal. An empath's natural inclination toward healing and helping others opens up a variety of career options. During the earlier chapters, you were introduced to the different strengths of an empath. Creating a career by using one of your strengths is a great way to harness your empathy and create a livelihood. This section looks at career choices that allow you to use your gift to help others.

Psychologist

Empaths make brilliant psychologists because they have a keen awareness of human nature and emotions. They are capable of understanding what others feel and can sense the reasons for these feelings. Mental health is as important as physical health. A mental health issue is as debilitating as a physical illness. These days, there is a growing demand for mental health specialists, and an empath is well suited to this role. Their inherent understanding of emotional suffering, coupled with the ability to help others, works brilliantly well in this field. They are also good at listening and offering helpful advice.

Nurse

Empaths are natural healers and caregivers. They are automatically drawn to anyone who is in pain. In fact, empaths often go out of their way to alleviate any suffering others are experiencing. Because of this natural desire to help others who are not well or ill, becoming a nurse is a good career option. A nurse is a healer, and it helps channel your empathy to reduce a patient's anguish. Working in nursing homes, hospitals, or even private houses allows you to use your empathy to comfort and soothe others.

Veterinarian

Empaths have an affinity toward animals. They feel deeply for nature and all its creatures, which is not just limited to human beings. It might seem surprising, but empaths are quite good at understanding what animals feel. You might have heard the term "horse whisperer" or an "animal whisperer." Well, that deep connection with nature allows an empath to understand the pain and suffering of other beings who cannot communicate as people do. It makes empaths feel deeply for them. Empaths make excellent vets because of their natural desire to heal and comfort sick pets.

Writer

Empaths are extremely creative. If you have a passion or a flair for writing, consider turning it into a full-time employment opportunity. Writing is a creative outlet to channel your feelings. Usually, empaths experience a variety of emotions foreign to them, and these emotions can trigger your creative juices and help you write. You can become an author, a freelance writer, or even a blogger. Allow your inner storyteller to come to the forefront and lose yourself in the journey. Writing can be a great escape from the world and is an excellent way for an empath to spend time alone.

Musician

As with writers, musicians are extremely emotional beings. If you have a knack for music and are an empath, consider turning it into a career opportunity. From writing songs or poetry to singing and even playing an instrument, there are different things you can consider. Beautiful music is composed by those who understand pain. Since an empath's heart naturally goes out to others, their understanding of pain and suffering is more heightened than others. In a way, you are using your strength as an empath to carve a career for yourself.

Artist

Empaths make excellent artists due to their boundless creativity. Writing can be used as a medium for an empath to express themselves, and art does the same. An empath's energy and imagination can be channeled through art using multiple media. It can be a video channel on YouTube showcasing your creativity, working as a freelancer, or even selling your artwork through online and offline portals. An empath's soul is attuned to the constant ebb and flow of human emotional currents, and creating art becomes meaningful to them.

Teacher

Teaching is one of the noblest professions known to humankind. A teacher's primary role is to guide their students toward success. Teachers inspire and push their disciples to excel in life and work toward their goals. Since empaths are all about uplifting the human spirit and collective progress, teaching becomes a good option. Their loving hearts, coupled with helping hands, make them an ideal candidate for this profession. Proper support and motivation can work wonders in one's life. A teacher is able to offer these things to their students, especially to those who do not get this at home.

Life Coach

Empaths thrive when happy people surround them. They are not jealous of others' success and, in fact, rejoice in this feeling. They also like helping others. Since they are excellent listeners and problem solvers, becoming a life coach is a great option. Helping others to become the best version of themselves will help put your empathy to good use. Since you always have the best interests of others at heart, being a coach will come naturally to you. If you have noticed most of your loved ones or acquaintances depend on you in their times of need for advice, it is all because of empathy and compassion.

Guidance Counselor

Just like teachers, even guidance counselors have the power to shape the life of a young adult. Guidance counselors act as mentors. Since empaths are great listeners and problem solvers, they often come up with brilliant advice. This is precisely the kind of advice a young adult needs during the formative years of their life. Also, this is a truly rewarding and fulfilling experience for the empath. As a counselor, you will be assisting pupils while working toward their endeavors, making sure they stay on the right track and pursue their goals. You will be required to offer them encouragement and motivation to explore opportunities that come their way. All these things come naturally to an empath, and it is a great way to channel your superpowers. Since empaths are good at understanding what others need—even if they do not understand themselves—working as a guidance counselor will be a fulfilling experience.

Social Service

Empaths like helping others and often go out of their way to do it. Since the world desperately needs empathy and compassion, social work is one avenue you must not overlook. It is personally rewarding, fulfilling, and uplifting. These are three things an empath always seeks in life. Whether you decide to become a social worker or work with a non-profit organization, there are different things you can do that will help you give back to society.

Empaths make a wonderful difference in every life they touch, and social work is a natural fit for you in this world. However, when it comes to social work, you need to be cautious. Empaths thrive on happiness and generally feel better about themselves if others are happy. If the story does not end well or things don't turn out for the better, it can take a toll on an empath's wellbeing. When you work with some of the worst-hit members of society or negative elements, you have to take care of your energy levels. If you take things too personally and let it consume you, your job will quickly overwhelm you. You will learn more about protecting and enhancing your energy as an empath in later chapters.

Hospice Worker

As with nurses and anyone else involved in the medical profession, becoming a hospice worker is another role to consider. Offering comfort and solace to dying patients and their family members will put your empathy to good use. Facing a life-threatening illness is seldom easy. It takes motivation and courage to work with such individuals. Hospice work involves elements of spirituality and social work. This work is quite appealing to an empath because it is not rigid and does not limit their abilities. You also have a chance to influence the mindset and moods of others around you. It helps channel your empathy to elevate grief.

Self-Employment Opportunities

Any form of self-employment is a good idea for an empath. If you are self-employed, it means you do not have to depend on others for your livelihood. You are your boss and can set your work schedule according to your needs and requirements. It gives you complete control and autonomy over your business operations. It also reduces any interactions with others, which are common in a typical corporate setting. Self-employment gives you a chance to explore your creative side and turn one of your passions into a paying form of employment. The tech-dominated world you live in has opened up new doors for self-employment opportunities. From drop shipping niche stores and online businesses, there are several avenues you can explore. Most of these businesses can be conducted from the comfort of your own home. Well, what more could an empath want?

Now that you know the different job opportunities available to you that will help harness your energy, certain jobs are not ideal for empaths. To enhance your empathic abilities, it is best to avoid jobs that drain your energy. For instance, any job where you constantly deal with others or the public, in general, can be extremely stressful. Some obvious jobs that are not suited for an empath include sales where you deal with customers or offer technical support, advertising, selling products, or marketing. Even being a cashier can feel overwhelming. If you are constantly in touch with others, you absorb their energy, feelings, and physical symptoms. Other career options that are not ideal for an empath include anything related to politics, public relationships, human resource management, and executives responsible for managing big teams. Becoming a trial lawyer will be emotionally exhausting too. However, certain branches of law will work well for an empath that requires the emotional maturity to deal with trying matters such as domestic violence or abuse. Any career that doesn't stimulate your creativity or imagination and requires an extroverted nature is not advisable.

Generally, the conventional corporate setup might not be the best choice either.

If you cannot change your job or if it is not ideal, you can take steps to make it more comfortable. Use the different shielding techniques discussed in the following chapters to protect your empathy and personal energy.

Chapter 10: How to Unlock Your Power as an Empath

As an empath, it is your responsibility to harness and unleash your inner power of empathy. It is a superpower, and you need to hone it. However, most empaths often concentrate on others and forget about themselves in this process. The more you do this, the more luster your empathy loses. Therefore, the first thing you need to do is work on yourself and improve your empathy skills. This section looks at simple tips you can follow to achieve this goal.

Acknowledge and Accept

If you want to unleash or unlock your true potential as an empath, the first step is to acknowledge and appreciate your gift. Most empaths live life without even being aware that they are empaths. Some struggle to accept their empathy. If you run away from your empathy or believe it is a burden, it will do you no favors. Instead, it will merely imbalance your life and make things difficult. Compassion is your true calling as an empath. Acknowledge that you are hardwired to help others and accept your empathy with open arms.

Once you accept your empathy, honing this gift becomes easier. This is the first step toward allowing your inner empath to shine bright. In the previous chapters, you were introduced to the various traits of an empath. If you notice those traits in yourself or experience any of the situations discussed earlier, you are an empath. Do not allow others to label you as "oversensitive" or "touchy." No, this is just a sign of your empathy. The sensitivity is something that others don't have. You are unique and special the way you are. Don't hide or run away from your gift. Instead, accept the truth that you are an empath.

No Self-pity

Empaths are extremely wonderful, but they lack self-awareness and have low levels of self-worth. Stop wallowing in self-pity and take steps to improve your self-confidence and self-worth. If left unchecked, an empath's need to be loved can create a victim mentality. Your empathy is not a weakness; it is your strength. It's the key to unlocking your true purpose in life. Most empaths are often overwhelmed because of their empathy, and it creates a variety of mental, physical, and spiritual imbalances. These imbalances make it easier for the empath to develop a victim mentality. Stop victimizing yourself and, instead, concentrate on the positive aspects of your life. Think about all the different instances when your empathy helped you. Whether it is your sense of intuition or imagination, it might have helped you at some point or another. Once you concentrate on the good things that empathy brings into your life, your self-worth will increase.

Trust Your Gut

Empaths have a strong sense of intuition because of their highly sensitive nature. You can understand what others feel or experience without needing verbal cues. You can see beyond this and know their true intentions. Any psychic images you receive, any signals you get from them, their energy vibrations, or the little voice in your head, listen to them. This is your empathy at play. If your gut says something is wrong, go with it. Chances are your gut is right. Have there been instances in your life when you made a decision, even when all logic defied it? Did a little voice tell you what to do? What were the outcomes in such instances? Were the outcomes positive and helpful? If you think about these examples, you will understand it was your intuition guiding the way. If your gut tells you something is wrong, something certainly is amiss. Work on improving your intuition and trust your gut. The more you trust your instincts, the more fine-tuned your intuition becomes. It also helps you stay away from toxic individuals and instead create healthy and positive relationships.

Establish Boundaries

This book repeatedly mentions that empaths need to establish personal boundaries. By now, you are probably aware that different people have different effects on you. Some individuals make you feel instantly happy while others drain you of all energy. Start paying attention to how you feel in certain situations and around people. If something feels off, something is definitely off about the situation.

Use your intuition to set limits and personal boundaries. The establishing of boundaries is a sign of self-esteem and self-respect. It lets you know the extent to which you can push yourself and when to stop. It also teaches others what is and is not acceptable to you. Don't just implement the boundaries, but also ensure there are consequences if the boundaries are violated. If you feel uncomfortable in a situation, it is a sign that one of your boundaries is compromised. With practice and conscious effort, you will finally understand when you are supposed to walk away for good and restore your empathy. It also helps you say "no" in the right situations and reduces stress. In turn, it gives you more time for yourself to concentrate on the activities you love and enjoy.

No Negative Energy

As an empath, you are an emotional sponge. You do not discriminate about the energy you absorb from others. It can be positive, negative, or anything in between. Whatever it is, you pick it up and carry it with you as with your energy. You need to stop doing this if you want to grow as an empath. Remember: There is only so much you can give to others without compromising yourself. It is not your responsibility or duty to fix everyone's problems. Help whenever possible, but that is about it. Don't take these energies or negative emotions on as if they are yours, and stop carrying this emotional baggage with you. All this increases any anxiety you feel and will worsen your overall mood. The first responsibility you have in life is toward yourself.

There are different techniques you can use to get rid of negative analogies in different situations. For instance, place plants at your workspace or home so they absorb negative energies. Similarly, you can use protective crystals such as amethyst or quartz to safeguard your personal energy field from unwanted energies. Another simple technique you can use is to change any negative thinking to positive thoughts. Always maintain a positive attitude in life, and it quickly dispels negativity. Spending time by yourself after a tiring day can also eliminate negative analogies that might be carried unknowingly. Try to look for humor in every situation and start your day with gratitude. Be grateful for all the good you have in life, and do not wallow in self-pity. If you want to, you can use positive affirmations to improve your quality of life in different aspects.

Healing Power of Breath

Whenever things start getting a little overwhelming for you, take a break from the situation. If you cannot walk away, channel all your energies inward. Concentrate only on yourself and your breathing. By shifting all your focus to your breathing, it helps reduce any stress you might be experiencing. It also gives you a better sense of control over the situation. It is easy to get overwhelmed, but it is tricky to regain control of yourself. The good news is you always have this power and choice. Don't let anyone or anything make you feel helpless. There is always a choice provided if you are willing to make it. Learn to breathe consciously and mindfully. Whenever you breathe in, visualize that you are breathing in the healing power of the universe and exhale all negativity energy present within and around you. Your breath is an incredibly powerful healing force.

If possible, head outdoors and practice this simple breathing exercise. Whenever you inhale, repeat the mantra, "I am breathing in positivity." When you exhale, repeat the mantra, "I am breathing out negativity and am filled with positivity." Do this exercise for a couple of minutes, and you will soon feel better about yourself. Taking a few deep breaths calms you down and expels any negative energy. Once your mind is free of stress and negativity, it becomes easier to think about the situation logically and rationally without getting overly negative.

Self-love

Your life's purpose is not to take care of others; it is about taking care of yourself. Self-love is quintessential for everyone, and even more so for empaths. You deserve the same empathy you reserve for others. Be compassionate toward yourself, your thoughts, and your emotions. Develop and follow a proper self-care routine and spend time taking care of your needs and requirements. Do not ignore any unprocessed feelings, and certainly do not suppress them. Be accepting of yourself to bring about a sense of positivity into your life.

Do not shy away from your emotions, and embrace all your sensitivities. Vulnerability is not a sign of weakness; it is your strength. Accept that you can be strong and vulnerable at the same time without any compromises. Don't forget to congratulate yourself whenever you listen to your intuition and something good comes out of it. Hold on to all the happy memories you have in life and try to amplify them. Don't allow negativity to bring you down. Love yourself unconditionally, and always be there for yourself. After all, you are the only one who will be there for you.

Meditation Helps

All empaths require downtime to recharge and recover. What happens to your smart phone's battery if you use it all day long? It might not have any charge left and will automatically turn off. Well, this is pretty much what happens to your energy levels if you do not recharge them. Using this analogy, meditation is similar to your phone's charger. There is a popular misconception that meditation is all about religion. No, it is a tool for spirituality. Spirituality and religion are two different concepts. You don't have to be religious to be spiritual.

Meditate for at least five to ten minutes daily, and you will see a positive change in your life. It is a great way to connect with the powerful energies of the universe while letting go of toxic energy. Meditation can make you feel grounded and centered. It relieves the sensory overload and gives your body, mind, and heart a much-needed break. While meditating, visualize. You are surrounded by a protective bubble that prevents toxic energy from reaching into your personal space. This bubble eliminates the unnecessary energy you soaked up during the day and replaces it with positive energy. Focus on this energy whenever you feel depleted.

Steps to Become a Skilled Empath

If you are tired of feeling like an overburdened and overwhelmed empath, it is time to regain control of your life. In this section, you will learn about seven phases you should go through to become a skilled empath.

Most empaths are stuck in the first phase, known as the *burdened phase.* Your sensitivity might feel like a severe weakness or a burden that is holding you down. Your empathy might feel like a deficiency. You are probably trying incredibly hard to prove to yourself and the world in general that you are tougher than they think. You are tired of feeling and experiencing everyone else's emotions. If you are in this phase, the first thing you need to do is accept that you are an empath. If you have progressed to this chapter, you have a pretty good idea of what empathy means and what life is like for an empath.

Now that you have accepted your gift, it is time to take care of yourself. The second phase is all about *basic self-care.* Take time to rest and recover. Avoid toxic environments or any situations that stimulate your senses. Accept and make peace with your high levels of sensitivity and empathy will not feel like a weakness. By now, you have probably realized the different circumstances and individuals who drain your energy.

The third phase is about *understanding your energies.* You can use meditation and visualization to cleanse your energy field and prevent the buildup of toxic energies. To do this, you need to become conscious of all your interactions. How do you feel when you meet certain people or go to particular places? Make a note of how you feel when you walk away from such individuals or locations. This simple practice will help you understand your personal energy levels and the effect others have on you. By now, you probably feel better about your empathy, but you get the sense that whatever you are doing isn't sufficient.

Well, this leads to the fourth stage when you need to *train your empathy.* You need to carefully and consciously reprogram your subconscious mind and thought patterns. It helps prevent the absorption of external feelings. You will see a positive change in your attitude toward yourself and the world. Once you consciously try to prevent absorbing others' emotions and thoughts, your energy fields will strengthen. It will make you feel lighter, and any mental fog you experienced during the earlier phases will fade away. You will feel more comfortable in your skin and accept the fact that you are an empath.

The fifth phase of becoming a skilled empath is to *control your energy fields*. During this stage, you realize how much more control you feel in situations where you do not take up others' feelings. It gives you time and energy to process your thoughts and emotions. This stage includes much self-reflection. You start understanding you have gifts that can be used to help others. At the same time, you also realize that it is not your responsibility to fix everyone else's lives. Take the required steps to accept the simple truth that you are responsible only for your thoughts, actions, feelings, etc. Take control of your daily life and love it on your terms.

If you keep practicing the different things you have learned in the previous phases, it brings you to the phase of *increased clarity*. By reprogramming your subconscious not to absorb unwanted energies or emotions, you come to a point where you are comfortable in crowds. You might not feel extremely comfortable, but you do not feel overwhelmed like you used to. If you still feel overwhelmed when in crowds, you probably need to practice managing your empathy. Constantly check in with yourself after you become exposed to intense energies from others. Even if you pick up something, in this stage, you have complete control over your energies to let go of things you don't want.

If you keep working on your empathy, you will finally reach the final phase of becoming a *skilled empath*. In this stage, even when you pick up others' energies or emotions, it does not overburden or overwhelm your senses. Your sensitivity is in check, and there will be days when you even forget you are an empath. You are finally in control and at peace.

Chapter 11: Shielding Techniques for Empaths

If you want to thrive as an empath, it is important to shield yourself from negative energies. Empaths are susceptible to excessive stimulation, exhaustion, and sensory overload. Therefore, the first thing you need to do is recognize when you are overstimulated and are experiencing any form of sensory overload. Start paying attention to when you absorb negative energy from others. By shielding and protecting your energies, you are essentially cleansing your aura. Your empathy is like a free Wi-Fi network. Anyone within the range of the signal of your Wi-Fi network can connect and use your data. Learning to make this network protected and selective is the simplest and securest way to ensure your energy field is not depleted. This section looks at practical techniques you can use to shield yourself from unwanted energies and emotions.

Shielding Visualization

Shielding is the quickest and most efficient way to protect yourself. What is the first thing that pops into your mind when you think of the word shielded? Probably medieval knights who were holding a shield to protect their bodies. Well, a shielding meditation does the same thing to your energy field. You are creating a barrier around yourself that prevents other energies from entering your aura. You can use this technique to block toxic energy and increase the free flow of positivity. Whenever you are uncomfortable in a situation, place, or around an individual, bring up your protective shield. Surround yourself with positive energy.

The great thing about this shielding visualization is you can do it whenever you want to, wherever you are. To get started, close your eyes and take a few deep breaths. While you do this, visualize a wonderful shield of bright white light surrounding your body. It extends from the tip of your toes to the top of your head, covering every inch of your external body. Keep visualizing this shield removing any unwanted energies present within and outside your body while blocking further toxic energy. Once you feel calm and centered, open your eyes, and end the meditation. Remember: This protective shield will stay with you throughout the day or until you need it. Call upon it whenever the need arises.

Protective Meditation

There will be instances when you need a little extra support to get through the day. In such cases, use the protective jaguar meditation. It is ideal for situations when there is too much negativity bombarding you. The jaguar is a patient, fierce, and protective guardian who keeps away toxic energy and individuals.

Close your eyes, take in a couple of deep breaths, and calm your mind. Once you are in the perfect meditative state, call upon the jaguar's spirit to guard you. Feel the jaguar enter your energy field. To do this, visualize the majestic creature in your mind's eye gracefully patrolling around you. While the jaguar is patrolling your energy field, it protects you, keeps away unwanted energy, and enhances your personal energy. Make your visualization of the jaguar as clear and precise as you possibly can. Visualize its eyes, graceful movements, powerful body, rippling muscles, and sleek movements. While the jaguar is encircling you, you are protected and safe. It will keep all things negative away from you. Place your trust in this creature, and thank it for its protection. Whenever you need it, you can call upon it, and it will protect you. Feel the power of this meditation, and let it stay with you throughout the day. Once you feel calm and secured, open your eyes, and get back to your usual routine.

Energetic Boundaries

In one of the previous chapters, you were introduced to the concept of setting energetic boundaries. Whether it is your home or office, create an energetic boundary around your personal space. It helps reduce any stress you experience and prevent negative energy from entering your sacred space. If you are constantly stuck in an environment that is crowded or emotionally challenging, fill your outer space with family photos, protective crystals, or plants. These objects help establish a psychological barrier similar to the effect of noise-canceling headphones.

Define and Express Your Needs

A simple form of self-protection is to acknowledge and understand your needs and assert them. Being assertive is not the same as selfishness. It essentially means you know what you want and are not afraid to ask for it. Once you learn to be assertive in any relationship, it gives you complete control over your situation and ensures a happy and well-balanced relationship. If something does not feel right to you, talk to your partner about it. Learn to define and express your needs in a relationship, especially the romantic ones. Instead of letting your negative emotions worry and consume you, communicate them. Finding the voice to stand up for yourself is similar to unleashing your superpower or empathy. Otherwise, others will take you for granted, and it will increase your anxiety. Remember, you are an empath, but it doesn't mean everyone else around you is as well. At times, all you need to do is ask or express yourself. Therefore, do not hesitate to do this. If you feel you are deprived of something, seek it instead of letting negative emotions overwhelm you.

Avoid Empathy Overload

Empathy overload is quite possible when you constantly absorb stress or any other symptoms others exhibit. Therefore, there is a need to let go of this negativity. The simplest way to prevent empathy overload is by spending time outdoors. Even if it is just for fifteen minutes daily, spending time outdoors is important. Learn to balance your need for alone time with the time you spend with other people. Time management is a skill that will come in handy for all empaths. Apart from this, learn to set limits, especially when you know you interact with toxic individuals. Learn to say "no" and do not feel guilty about it. Saying "no" is a complete sentence, and you don't need to offer explanations to anyone. If something doesn't feel right, trust your gut and go with it.

Breathe Out Negativity

If you feel sad, low, anxious, or experience any physical discomfort for no apparent reason, it is likely that all these things are not *your* feelings. If you feel uncomfortable around a specific individual or place, it is a sign of negativity. Listen to your intuition in such situations. Here is a simple breathing exercise you can perform to let go of any negativity. Close your eyes and concentrate only on your breathing for a couple of minutes. Take long and slow breaths and exhale slowly. As you inhale, imagine you are breathing in all things good and exhaling the uncomfortable energy. Breathing helps push negativity out of your body.

Whenever you do this breathing exercise, here is a simple mantra you can repeat. For best results, repeat it three times and in a tone that says you mean business. You can say it out loud or even repeat it mentally. The mantra is, "Return to the sender, return to the sender, return to the sender." Channel your inner empathy and send the unwanted energy back to the universe. While repeating this mantra, concentrate on your lower back region. This place often acts as a conduit for negative energy. When you focus on this region and breathe out while repeating this mantra, it helps your breath eliminate the toxic energy you were experiencing.

Question Your Feelings

If you notice a sudden change in your mood, energy, or feelings, it is a sign that you are absorbing someone else's energy. If you were not feeling sad, anxious, or exhausted before the internal discomfort or turmoil, it might be that the energy you are absorbing is not yours but that of others around you. Whenever you notice this subtle change in yourself, question your feelings. Instead of accepting them as yours, challenge them. There is no space for other things in life if you are not comfortable in your skin. If the other person is experiencing an issue similar to the one you are going through and has not figured it out yet, the feelings or symptoms you experience are further magnified. Don't let this happen to yourself, and learn to identify whose emotions you are feeling. If the unsettling emotions you are experiencing are not yours, send them away. You can use the meditation technique discussed in the previous points to do this.

Take a Step Back

If you suspect that something or someone is negatively affecting you, take a step back from the suspected source. Move at least twenty feet away and notice how you feel. You do not have to worry about offending strangers. Instead, concentrate on your energy levels. Saying "no" to certain energies is perfectly fine and is a form of self-protection. For instance, if you are seated in a restaurant next to a rather noisy group, change your seating arrangement, or even leave if you feel uncomfortable. Additionally, don't forget to focus on yourself. If you keep trying to please others or are worried about offending others, you cannot live life to the fullest. Permitting yourself to step away from the situation that is disturbing you is a form of self-care and self-preservation. Social settings can be extremely overwhelming for an empath. Therefore, don't hesitate to take a break from all these things. Once you have replenished your energies, it is entirely up to you whether you want to return to the situation or not.

Detox with Water

Water helps eliminate negative energy and dissolve stress. The simplest way to protect and preserve your analogy is by taking a leisurely bath. An Epsom salt bath is a wonderful way to calm yourself. It also provides magnesium, which has a calming effect. To enhance the overall harmonious effect, you can add a couple of drops of soothing essential oils, such as lavender, to the bathwater. A relaxing bath at the end of a tiring day will make you feel refreshed. Plus, a nice bath is a great bedtime ritual, as a soothing bath can enhance your sleep quality. To make things extra special, you can light a few scented candles and soak in the water's goodness.

Connect with Nature

Empaths are drawn to nature and love it. Nature makes them feel safe and at home. It gives you a chance to connect with your inner self without any worries or prejudices. The way water clears negativity, spending time in nature has a similar effect. Reconnecting with nature helps heal energy deficiencies you are experiencing. It also helps eliminate negative energy and replaces it with pure positivity. Walk on the grass and stand barefoot for a while. Let your feet be in direct contact with the earth and its healing energies. Being barefooted has a grounding effect on an empath. Maintain direct contact with the ground until you feel settled and restored.

Do not forget to express your gratitude once the earth's healing energy has helped you. Keep doing this daily, and you will see a positive change.

All the different shielding techniques discussed in this section are simple but take practice. With consistent practice, time, and effort, you will get the hang of it. Even if you do not succeed immediately, don't worry; keep practicing. Sensory overload is quite common, and if you don't want to feel exhausted and are anxious because of someone else's energies, protect yourself. Take charge of your life and your sensitivities. You don't have to be victimized; instead, learn to regulate your feelings.

Chapter 12: The Role of Empaths in Today's World

"What is my purpose in life?"

"What is my purpose as an empath on this earth?"

Most empaths struggle to answer these two common questions, especially when they are learning to embrace their empathy and harnessing their power. In fact, most people wonder about our life's purpose and the role they are meant to play. This question might sound deeply personal and even spiritual to a certain extent. After all, everyone wants to be a part of something big or know that their life has meaning, and they are not merely whiling away their time on this planet. The longer this question is left unanswered, the more frustrating it becomes. This frustration is magnified for an empath. It is equally frustrating to acknowledge that you are blessed with a gift that others do not have, yet you don't know what you're supposed to do with it. Not knowing what the gift is meant for or what you can do with it can be extremely troubling and tiring for an empath.

As an empath, you are well aware of your inherent desire to help others. Empaths love to help others and society in general. However, they easily get overwhelmed if they spend prolonged periods around too many people. This, in turn, makes it harder to determine their life's purpose. The desire or basic need to be of service to others is an inherent characteristic of all empaths. Usually, this stems from some suffering empaths endure during a certain phase in their lives. Since they have experienced some pain, it increases their urge to alleviate any anguish others might experience. This, coupled with an empath's need to be of service, makes it even more important for an empath to determine their purpose in life.

It is okay to try to help others, but there is an important lesson every painful experience teaches you in life. It is equally important to let people live their lives without coming to their rescue whenever you notice any suffering. Certain lessons are meant to be learned, and unless they learn these lessons, they will keep repeating the same patterns. All suffering is not necessarily bad, and there is a silver lining to even the darkest of clouds. Suffering has helped humans evolve. It acts as a reality check that awakens and prompts them to look for a new and better life path. Suffering can also be a source of spiritual enlightenment and awakening. No matter the anguish people have endured, they need direction and a sense of purpose. You might want to help others find the right direction or path for themselves; however, this is a personal decision, and all you can do is help them when they need it.

All empaths are unique, and what might be right for one is not necessarily right for someone else. Therefore, do not get overwhelmed, don't worry about others, and learn to concentrate on yourself first. Develop an acute sense of self-awareness and empathy before reaching out to others. Many empaths believe they cannot serve their life's true purpose if they don't work with others. Well, this is the part where it gets tricky. As an empath, spending a lot of time with people is not possible because it becomes emotionally and mentally overwhelming.

A simple truth you need to accept is that you do not always have to be of service to others directly. You can indirectly help others too. There are several behind-the-scenes jobs you can take on to do your bit for society. When it comes to an understanding of your empathy, learn to listen to your gut. Trust your intuition and let it guide you. The answer to "What's my life purpose as an empath?" is not something that you can discover overnight. It is a journey of self-discovery. Stop being hard on yourself and learn to be patient. The universe has something in store for everyone.

You probably have not even realized it, but you do more for others than you give yourself credit for. Helping others doesn't necessarily mean making their lives better. It can be as simple as listening to them when they need to be heard or giving them the time and space required for healing. Listening is also a great way of healing. These days, most people are busy talking all the time and rarely have any time to listen. They are busy thinking about their stories and what they need to do next. In such a world, empaths are truly a rare breed of excellent listeners. They do this not just because they want to, but also because they care. As mentioned, you are probably helping others in more ways than you realize. Therefore, stop worrying and don't be critical of yourself.

If you want to make the world a better place, concentrate on healing yourself first. Make yourself a better person, and you have already done your bit for society. When it comes to finding your life's purpose, listen to your heart, and go with your intuition. However, before you can start doing this successfully, it is important to understand your energies and keep them well balanced. If your empathy is imbalanced, you will feel anxious, overwhelmed, and depressed. If you have accepted your empathy and have gained a sense of balance and control over it, interacting with others becomes easier. An unbalanced empath's energy is often distorted, and their intuitive responses are limited.

An underlying health condition, undiagnosed disorders, food intolerance, or inability to shield your energy are common reasons why your empathy is not balanced. In such instances, how you interpret your intuition and react to those around you is also different. If any physical or mental ailments weaken you, you cannot function optimally as an empath. It also reduces any inclination you have toward helping others. Therefore, it is important to put your oxygen mask on before you go about helping others. You cannot help anyone, let alone yourself, if you do not understand your empathy.

The good news is that this problem can be easily fixed. You have complete control over your life, even when you do not understand it right now. You have the power to accept and reject any energy or emotions you experience. No one else has control over this. Stop feeling helpless and powerless. It is time to regain control of your life. Follow the simple and practical tips and techniques discussed in the previous chapters about protecting your energy while harnessing its power. Take care of yourself and develop a good self-care regimen.

Do not push yourself and stop believing you are a tireless machine. Develop your intuition, shield your energy, calm your mind, and get rid of unnecessary stress. By doing this, you will feel more balanced and energetic. It also helps determine your reason and purpose as an empath. Remember: Your calling is not just to help others; it is also to enjoy your time on this planet. People are not immortal, so learn to enjoy a mortal life. Stop getting obsessed with the idea of helping others to the extent that you forget about yourself in this process. Just because you are an empath doesn't mean you need to suffer to alleviate others' suffering constantly. You are doing yourself a grave injustice. Know yourself and respect your empathy. It is a gift which you should learn to cherish. At the same time, learn to establish and implement boundaries that prevent you from going overboard.

The little voice in your head, which keeps telling you to reduce others' pain, is a calling from your soul. It essentially tells you that something is not right, and you need to change. You have complete power to be the change you want to see in the world. It is never too late to change the direction of your life.

Many believe that empathy is a gift from the universe to help humanity. An empath's keen sense of intuition and understanding of human suffering compels them to do their bit for the world. Take time for self-reflection, meditate, and concentrate on answering the important questions you have about your life. Go through your character traits and all the abilities you have and note different ways to be of service to others. Your unique talents and an open and giving heart are the gifts the world needs right now. Once you harness and truly understand your empathy, living life as an empath becomes easy. It also helps you see the bigger picture and understand how you fit in.

Conclusion

Enjoying your life to the fullest or leading a carefree existence can become tricky if you struggle with empathy. Try to understand that empathy is a beautiful and unique gift only a lucky few are blessed with. Empaths often run into difficulties and challenges in their daily life because they struggle to accept their gift of empathy. Unless you understand, recognize, and embrace your gift with open arms, living life as an empath will not be easy. Recognize your blessings, and your life will become wonderful. Instead of feeling that something is missing in your life, concentrate on the good aspects. The first step is to accept your gift of empathy and work to enhance it.

In this book, you were given all the information you need to understand empathy, recognize your strengths, overcome weaknesses, and truly harness the powers of empathy. Improving and strengthening your skills is as important as shielding it from energy vampires and narcissists. Unless you do this, chances are your personal energy field will be quickly depleted, and you will be left feeling overwhelmed and uneasy. By understanding your abilities, it becomes easier to empower and heal yourself. After all, you cannot help others unless you have helped yourself first. Therefore, it is time to take control of your life and start following the simple advice presented in this book.

Now that you have discovered how to avoid common mistakes empaths make, you can now establish strong and healthy relationships and find the best way to utilize your power. Empathy is a superpower that you must accept. The sooner you do this, the easier it becomes to harness your gift. As with anything else in life, it is quintessential that you are patient and considerate toward yourself. The empathy you reserve for others should also be directed toward yourself. By following the helpful information given in this book, you will be a step closer to attaining the inner peace you desire. Remember: The key to your happiness lies in your hands. Unless you give this power away to someone else, no one else can take it from you.

While using the practical tips and techniques in this book, be patient, compassionate, and understanding toward yourself. Heal yourself as an empath and unleash the potential of your empathy. You have the power to help change the world.

Part 2: Highly Sensitive People

The Hidden Power Of a Person Who Feels Things More Deeply And What an HSP Can Do To Blossom

Introduction

It's great that you made the decision to crack the cover of this highly enlightening book. You'll be privy to some undoubtedly unusual and different perspectives than those already circulating about Highly Sensitive Persons (HSP).

You have noticed there is a difference between living and being alive. Meanwhile, to better understand this aspect of life as regards to being an HSP, you will be exposed to several scenarios that vividly clarify and clear up your doubts about certain issues.

It's okay to be perplexed about where you fall in the world of personalities, but you are sure to reach a solid conclusion once you go through the first chapter where you are guided through understanding the traits and habits that constitute a highly sensitive personality. This will help clear things up for you.

Get ready to relate deeply with experiences you might have come across while also gaining an extensive knowledge of strange or new experiences with your feelings and your dealings with people.

It doesn't matter if you're a beginner. The book is written simply and comprehensively to help even the least knowledgeable individuals understand the highly sensitive personality.

It should come as no surprise when you find yourself viewing certain scenarios and concepts in a different light. The book, unique from others, discusses the innermost feelings and traits of the highly sensitive.

It does not leave you to your thoughts. Instead, it guides you through every stage to help you better understand why a particular feeling *IS what it is.*

Go deeper, reflect, and connect and get ready to be a better sensitive person who doesn't just move as situations demand, but someone who thrives and sails towards personal development against all odds.

Chapter 1: Are You a Highly Sensitive Person?

My best guess is that you're working through this book trying to discover more about yourself or someone else who you think could fit into the description of a Highly Sensitive Person (HSP). But – what, exactly, does that term mean?

Most of the time, people progressing through one psychological condition or the other barely know it, and only a few fully know what it entails and how to handle it. This book offers a quick chance to learn if this label applies to you.

Dr. Elaine Aron coined the term "Highly Sensitive Person" in the 90s, and about 20% of the world's population has this trait. This is a character with a heightened central nervous system. This means he/she feels things (both physically and emotionally) more than others and responds to both internal and external stimuli.

Science sees a typical HSP as a person with Sensory Processing Sensitivity. This mostly concerns the brain, rather than just your senses. This trait is not like Spiderman's sixth sense, but more about your brain's ability to deal with material more intensely.

Do you find yourself being susceptible to loud sounds, bright lights, or strong scents? Do you process information deeply before you respond? Do you feel emotions (both yours and those of others) strongly, or are you more sensitive to the effects of caffeine, alcohol, medication, pain, or hunger? If yes, you should be interested in this journey of discovery.

Something very remarkable is that HSPs are born that way; it is an innate and genetic attribute rather than a medical or psychological diagnosis. This means this trait is not a problem or defect, but just like having blonde hair or blue eyes, it comes with its perks and downsides.

A Highly Sensitive Person (HSP) could be mistaken for an Empath or someone with autism, but their traits don't revolve around empathy alone. While autism and HSP may overlap in many areas, they are different.

The best thing for you is to tick the correct boxes yourself, so you're not just taking someone else's word for it, but you can learn where you fit into the spectrum.

Let's delve into what makes an individual sensitive.

1. Aware Of Subtle Happenings

This is easily one of the most notable features of somebody with this ability. Since your senses are heightened, you notice a change in different aspects of the environment, like slight sounds, décor, scents, and emotions. Besides just noticing these changes, you often react to them.

From the scent of fresh coffee that fascinates you almost as much as the coffee itself, to the uncomfortable feeling you have when you are in a room that's half-painted, you take the whole experience wherever you find yourself, as an HSP.

The reason is that your mind is reacting differently and has more insula. This is the part of the brain that enhances self-awareness.

From careful observation, HSPs will stop what they are doing and think about their next move more than those who are less engaged. They do not act in that moment, but need time to digest whatever problem faces them.

The reason is they are taking in more information from their environment and their contact with other people. They sense more and need to digest all of this. So, if you think you "feel too much" or "take matters too much to heart," you may just be a Highly Sensitive Person; but that's not all.

2. Have A Strong Dislike for Violence and Cruelty

Because they feel things more deeply than others do, they are often more triggered by any form of violence or cruelty. It's simple, their tolerance levels for assault are very low because they don't only sense it, but seem to be *experiencing* it as well.

If you're an HSP, you may not be able to sit through a whole war movie without feeling sick to your stomach or traumatized, simply because you go through the pain of the victims as if it is yours. Even though tolerance levels for violence vary among different HSPs, they are generally low.

This could occur based on these reasons:

- Your mirror neurons (the part of the brain that enables people to perceive what they watch) are more active. It means that whenever you witness activities, you experience them as if they were happening directly to you.

- You don't just observe, you also understand. Someone with a highly sensitive mind experiences the world with strong and distinct passions. This affects your reactions to what you see or watch. Gory sights will not only scare you, but will make you feel terrible and uncomfortable as an HSP.

- The emotions last longer than the occurrence. While plenty of people might be immediately startled when watching a horror movie or experiencing a frightening situation, they get over it soon after, but this is not the case. For them, moving on from such instances is nearly impossible. They are most likely to feel the emotional effects for a long time. They may discover themselves feeling such painful sentiments several years later when someone or something reminds them of the event.

- It can affect your slumber. Anything that takes your sleep away must be bad for your body and lifestyle. Everybody needs sleep, but they realize sleep very is important because they need to rest and recharge for the next day and all the sensitivity that comes with it. If witnessing a gory event or watching terrifying movies takes away from your rest period (because you repeatedly process the information you received), it's time to reconsider horror movies and disconcerting situations.

- You don't get to turn it off. Many people are gifted with the skill to block out what they don't want to interact with - sounds, sights and everything between. You'll find that this ability directly clashes with the ability to sense any and everything, so they don't get the choice of just blocking out the images they've seen. Their brain keeps replaying the events, and it could be traumatizing, so it is clear why violence triggers a lot.

3. Perform Poorly Under Time Pressure

Being pressured from a life stance can also form problems for someone who suffers from this, as the stimulation they suffer from stems from many sources. The intensity of having to do things within a set timeframe will make them much more sensitive.

Typically, they are overanxious when undertaking a task with a deadline. Even basic decision-making is often very draining for them because of all the thought, then having to do all that with a schedule in mind becomes frightening.

The pressure that comes with being given a deadline could certainly hamper the progress of the task completely. At this point, you begin to doubt yourself and your abilities to deliver, and probably imagine the worst-case scenario (that you cannot deliver the quality expected from you within the expected time).

Dr. Elaine Aron, the author of the book 'The Highly Sensitive Person,' confirms that often they struggle when dealing with deadlines and people putting pressure on them to complete a task. This is because of the depth of thought you give to the process.

You may notice yourself overthinking and thus discover that you lose track of time or even notice your mind is being overstimulated when you have a lot going on around you.

4. Perceptive

When you think deeply about details, you are prone to understand them better and therefore tackle those situations better than the alternatives. They find it easy to figure these ideas out because they hardly ever see them as surface values. When looking at a piece of art, you do not just look and say, "Whoa, it's beautiful!" but you want to discover what technique was used, why, and what message the artist was trying to convey.

Others see this as being insightful and seek help and advice from those around you with this skill. This is even more pronounced in extroverted people with this ability because they are more vocal with their opinions and will share their in-depth thoughts with anyone else who will listen.

5. Keeping To Oneself

It is one of two factors; you either understand the desire to take a break from the parts that trigger you, or you want to recharge your inner strength, which seems constantly dwindling. Just hang in there—the reason for that is coming up right now. Keeping to oneself does not mean you are an introvert, though. You usually feel the demand for time to process material.

The scientific explanation for HSPs needing a lot of space, according to Dr. Aron, is that the brain of this population processes knowledge more deeply while relating and comparing it to similar information received before. And this will be daunting because it's just like thinking up several recipes for the same meal repeatedly. So, it is essential to get enough downtime (preferably alone) to recuperate from "overstimulation" and digest your experiences. With this skill, you don't always prefer to be in the middle of the action.

6. Absorbing Other People's Emotions

Think of yourself as a sponge that cannot help but soak in other people's moisture (in this case, their desires), leaving you soaked and unable to go about your business like you want to. This is exactly the case of an HSP.

You can easily sense the mood of those in your surroundings without them having to tell you, and this often compels you to get into that mood, meaning when others around you are happy, so are you, and when their mood switches, so do yours.

7. Low Pain Tolerance

Understanding why HSPs are very sensitive to pain is simple: since they are overwhelmed with different emotions, physical pain is the last thing they'd want to experience, and once they do, it's almost impossible to handle the situation.

Whether it is the prick of a needle or an all-too-painful tap on your back, you notice it a lot more than another would, which could earn you the tag of being "too weak" or "dramatic," but it is normal for HSPs. Besides, you feel things more deeply than others do, so the pain is magnified.

8. Easily Scared

They are naturally very jumpy, and it takes little to startle them. It is called having a high "startle reflex" because, even in calm situations, their nerves are on a roll. It takes just a touch to spark a jerk from them. Also, loud or sudden sounds are bound to trip them up.

If you have this trait, it might be one reason for your complete hatred of any form of violence or cruelty. An HSP's mind does not want to unravel scary events in movies or any other means, which can easily be avoided.

9. Reacts To Stimulants

HSPs are naturally very sensitive to the consumption of caffeine, alcohol, drugs, or other stimulants. This is because their nervous system is already geared upwards, so just a little intake of stimulants could stir up more of a buzz than intended.

An HSP once confessed to being addicted to caffeine, but the only difference between her and other caffeine addicts was that every time she took a cup of coffee, she was extremely bubbly (like while on a substance high). When the effects wore off, she would be as tired as someone who had had no sleep, even after eight solid hours of sleeping, so she had to keep repeating the cycle. She was not only tired, but she was also emotionally drained and almost depressed when she had to give up her addiction.

The caffeine meant to keep you awake and mentally alert will induce unacceptable stress response levels, and since your levels are already naturally high, it just increases your anxiety and agitation. How much more stimulation can you take?

10. Deep Thinker

Most of the time, HSPs go beyond the surface to assess situations and people. This comes from their habit of reflecting on life experiences in a way that others may overlook. Still, because these elements automatically trigger stimulation, they'll notice themselves analyzing and processing information deeply.

As an HSP, you also think about things repeatedly. It could be a soccer game you watched with your friends, and you go over the details of the game repeatedly—the goals, chances, assists, penalties, and even the cards given out by the referee.

The downside to that is it could lead to negative overthinking, which could prevent you from making decisions that would help you.

11. Creative/ Visionary Thinker

Besides processing information deeply, they are very imaginative. For children, they most likely have imaginary friends or an imaginary world inside their heads where they go to escape the realities of life or generally feel more alive.

For adults, it could translate to daydreaming or ideating beyond the physical circumstances, like imagining the setup of your own company while still employed as an assistant at an organization. This could help with information processing and planning, especially if overthinking does not come in and steal the show.

12. Meticulous

This could also stem from being a deep and careful thinker. Someone with this skill is more meticulous than any other person. You more than likely show extreme care for even minute details.

They care about how their decisions may have an impact, and how other people's decisions affect them. They sometimes care about how others may perceive their actions because they are bound to think things through and through. It is a never-ending cycle of "what if's," "why's," "when's" and "how's."

13. Struggles With Change

Being an HSP, one would naturally prefer being around the same people and environments because, at least, you know what to expect from the familiar. So, a change in these variables will most likely trigger reactive feelings that are negative. They are also so used to their schedules and routines that an adjustment to this could distort their whole thought processes, and other aspects, for example their attitude and concerns.

14. Misunderstood

A typical HSP is usually misunderstood because other individuals can't seem to fathom why their reactions are "more dramatic" than "normal" people. High sensitivity is sometimes given other names such as being shy, anxious, or antisocial, but this is not the case. They find that their nerves are often on edge. It is confusing to try to explain to others when you're only just trying to figure out why your mind works in that way.

Dr. Elaine Aron, a psychologist and key contributor to HSP research, said one of her patients was labeled mentally challenged by people she cared about, to the point where she believed it, and started questioning her sanity.

If you feel as though many of these traits describe your personality, then you are probably a Highly Sensitive Person, but even if you can only relate to just a few, you could also be one. Just like every other trait inherent in humans (an example is being a blonde or a left-handed person), they vary in their levels of expression and exhibition but have habits that revolve around those mentioned here.

By now, ticking the right boxes should have given you closure on whether you're an HSP, and you are ready to get into the next phase of this journey.

Chapter 2: The Pros and Cons of Being an HSP

Now that you have either identified as a Highly Sensitive Person or discovered that you are not, you need to know that the trait is not a negative one, but, just like almost every other thing on this Earth, there are two sides to the story. People, including HSPs, tend to focus more on the negatives, but high sensitivity is not a bad thing.

It does not mean that one is weak or dramatic; it also doesn't mean that one has mental problems. It simply manifests as the ability to feel and process information more deeply than others, which could mean many things, including positivity.

Focusing only on the positives would not only be impractical but also potentially harmful. They should know that their traits have their downside, but they can manage them well when they have the facts they need.

Anyone who wants to understand how to maximize this trait should first know and understand the positive and negative aspects to it, and make them work for their own good. In the same way, to know how to deal with them so that they will be open to, you need to understand the good and the not so good in a more comprehensive way.

The Pros

These are the strengths associated with being a Highly Sensitive Person. It has been discovered that processing information intensely comes with its benefits, even though they might be too busy trying to figure themselves out to even notice or harness them. Life should be experienced in its totality, which is why you need to know these benefits for yourself.

1. Attention to Detail

The ability of HSPs to pay close attention to minuscule details quickly helps them spot things that could go wrong and try to change them. They also find it easy to read people's slightest emotions during conversations or general interactions.

This trait makes them great employees, friends, and colleagues. They know when there is something wrong with a friend, even if he/she is not willing to open up about it, and they try to make things right. They are also quick to notice a loophole in a contract that could prove to be an issue. While people may not see the need for this ability, it comes in handy during your lifetime, and it is one trait they have in abundance. They do not even have to try.

AN HSP does not overlook what can still be improved on. Some call this being "a perfectionist," but it results from sensitivity to subtle incidents rather than wanting to impress.

2. Creative

The care and thoughtfulness they put into their work does not stop their creativity from revealing itself. Rather, it gives it a boost. Because they have an inner world filled with so much life, their creativity bursts forth effortlessly.

They tend to use their imagination, and their thoughtfulness helps to give the direction of their ideas and can translate into something beautiful and meaningful. For example, an HSP writer puts more care into the meaning of each word to help the reader understand better and enjoy the work. His/her active imagination can help create a beautiful story that keeps the reader glued to what they are reading and wanting more.

Also, children who are HSPs could take experiences they have had, mix them with their ideals, and create imaginary worlds in their heads that help make playtime an enjoyable affair.

3. Gratitude For Little Things

This trait is something good that comes from paying close attention to detail. You can find them complimenting an Event Planner on the choice of cutlery or tablecloth at a party (things that others may not even notice). Also, they know of nature, and just watching the rising or setting of the sun could give one vast fulfillment, as opposed to just a "photo-worthy" memory others might take it for.

Even little gestures of love or kindness do not go unappreciated by them. A delightful kiss on the forehead or a reassuring squeeze of the palm could be all they need to see the light at the end of the tunnel. Hearing a beautiful melody could bring back a cherished memory that makes one grateful for life and everything it offers. To sum it up, they savor each moment.

4. Empathy

Even though it has been proven that empathy is not an HSP trait, it is a very notable feature of them that concerns their ability to feel others' emotions as if they were their own. Since the typical HSP is a more intentional and intense information processor, signals like a weak smile, sudden loss of appetite, unusual quietness, or a nervous hand gesture from someone else could immediately trigger an SOS call in the mind of an HSP. They will then try to make sure that they can help the person with whatever they are facing.

If we are honest, that is the friend everyone wants, someone you do not have to tell your problems before they try to work out a solution, and someone who can relate to the pains you're feeling, even without experiencing them before.

5. Self-Awareness

Naturally, if you are highly sensitive, you will also turn out to be very self-aware. Whether it starts right from the beginning of time or happens somewhere along the way, they develop the critical ability to look at themselves. This is because they tend to think deeply about things. They want to know why they feel things the way they do and why others can't seem to relate.

Those born with the innate ability to sense emotions more deeply find themselves more tuned in to their own emotions. They can look at themselves without bias and understand why others might not relate to what they are going through.

They easily sense they feel things differently from others, and this makes them more aware of their uniqueness. This situation also helps them know how to open up to others about their sensitive side to help others better understand them.

6. Ability to Bond

Although they are not close to many people, they know how to form bonds with those they find worthy. It may take a while for them to open up to others, but once they do, they know how to nurture their relationships, especially because of their empathic nature.

Also, because they are self-aware, they value individuals who allow them to express themselves when they are together. This is how it works. You know anybody willing to understand and relate to you - without making it feel weird - values you, and so you tend to give him or her that energy right back. This scenario also adds to the list of reasons why they are a great choice when looking for friends.

The Cons

We cannot deceive ourselves by thinking there is only one angle to anything. So, to strike a balance, you need to know the downsides so you can work around them, either as an HSP or someone who wants to know more about them. These are inherent traits you can't change, but you should learn how to make the most of them. Yes, it is possible to make the most of negative things, but first learn what they are.

1. Excessive Crying

Even though they do not want to be seen as "cry-babies" (I mean, who does?), they come off like this because they are always overwhelmed by emotions.

Whether it is a starry-eyed scene in a movie or a bad day at work, emotional situations are more overwhelming for them.

2. Mood Swings

This is one area where they are very misread. It takes little to change their attitude from positive to sorely downcast for those who feel things easily and deeply. The mood of the environment and the surrounding individuals easily trigger similar emotions from them, and this is not always pleasant.

Imagine a friend of yours, who laughed throughout the comedy movie you both just watched, suddenly giving you silent treatment after receiving a call. Then, he tells you he has to leave without explanation - when he *promised* to sleep over at your place. Your initial reaction might be shocked as to the sudden change in his mood.

Let's say you decide to call him because you want to know what happened, and he tells you that his project supervisor called to inform him that the deadline for his submission has been moved up, so he had to leave to continue working on it. You reassure him that all will be fine and say goodbye.

What you might not know is that the call disoriented him and crushed his joyful spirit, so he had to recoil into his shell to think up his next line of action (which was when he was not talking to you) and then opt to leave to work in an environment where he would not be distracted. He did not know how better to handle the situation, because his emotions were all over the place. The difference is that you do not see the big deal in what happened, because you have had many deadline changes before, but never freaked out that way.

To many people, it might seem like they are unstable or just can't take things lightly. Well, it is hard to do that when your emotional antenna is all over the place. This is just one example of this.

3. Decision Making

Deciding always seems like the most daunting task for the typical HSP. This is because of the tendency to overthink things. From choosing a snack for lunch to deciding on a career path for life, they are usually drained from weighing and re-weighing their options repeatedly. This experience could help you understand each option's dynamics, but it could also be completely unnecessary for something so insignificant. Although remember, they take note of EVERYTHING!

When what others may see as a trivial decision gets you all freaked out because you do not want to make a mistake, you are not just seen as different, but you might be losing out on the thrill of taking a risk. Life is not always about calculated moves and perfection, but exploring the different facets of the journey without being afraid to make mistakes. After all, they are part of the package.

Some have even called this a phase of "decision paralysis'" A few of the reasons why they overthink decisions include:

- They are deep processors. One of the four characteristics of HSPs that Dr. Aron highlights is that they process information very deeply. Hence, every piece of information associated with the decision process tends to be assessed repeatedly, delaying the process from actualizing. They do not take things or decisions at face value. They must dig in and unravel everything before they can decide on anything.

- They want to get the most out of everything. When they discover information, they want to get more information about it to decide whether it is useful or not. Considering that each piece of information is duly processed before moving ahead, not surprisingly, decision-making is a drag for them.

They want the best value from everything (based on their attention to details), and the only way to know which choice this is, is to discover everything about everything.

- They consider others. The empathy inherent in the typical HSP pushes them toward considering how their decisions affect other people. Questions like "Will my choice for a beach hangout affect anyone's schedule?" or "Can I wake up to read at night without disturbing my wife?" constantly boggle the minds of HSPs and sometimes stop them from doing what they would otherwise have done.

- They tend toward perfection. The attention to detail makes them want to do everything perfectly, but this is not even feasible because nothing is perfect. Those individuals on the ride to mission impossible take a long while before getting to their station, and sometimes, they don't even get there.

- They may not be confident in themselves. Those who are used to being misinterpreted and misunderstood might not even believe in their ability to make good decisions, which leads to more overthinking and even giving up.

4. People Pleaser

They automatically have a different upbringing than others. While many youths may recall how they loved going to the park when they were younger, many could not relate to that. This makes keeping up with conversations about shared experiences hard to have. So many turn to people-pleasing to form friendships and other relationships.

As an HSP, sometimes you just can't seem to handle criticism, so you try to make everyone get along with you. You do this in the hope of them approving your personality and actions, and this could take a toll on you.

This differs from being a naturally friendly person keen to form bonds. This (friendly) person also knows friendship is a give and take relationship. In fact, so is every other type of relationship.

As an HSP, you could also be interested in people-pleasing because you want everyone around you to be happy. When you put other individual's thoughts and feelings above yours on a consistent basis, it starts to weigh heavily on you, especially when they are not appreciative of your efforts. This could be devastating to the psyche.

To sum it up, the need to please others comes when they try to fit into a group where they are not like the other members of that group, and for them, it happens often.

5. Easily Misunderstood

Most the points mentioned above add up to explain why they can be misunderstood. This is the least favorable to the typical sensitive soul because it is hard enough having to deal with all the other difficulties that come with being highly sensitive. Then, just knowing that people do not understand how you feel and the way you reason is enough to destabilize you.

For each feature of HSP, there is a wrong notion that "explains" it.

- Their attention to detail is seen as petty and overbearing.

- While individuals might appreciate their creative thinking process, others may see it as wishful thinking or being unrealistic.

- Being grateful for the little things or appreciating the tiniest detail of nature could come off as being unnecessary.

- Mood swings could make you look unstable or melancholy, which might not always be the case.

- Those who are people pleasers could be seen as desperate for love or codependence.

- Those being easily prone to fear could come off as weak to many people.

Chapter 3: HSP vs. Empath

You would probably agree that when you are trying to explain a new word to another person, they might mention similar terms they are more conversant with, and ask you, "You mean like a...?" That's the power of similar concepts.

They – HSPs and Empaths - easily worm their way into other's heads (since they are based on previous knowledge) and are sometimes mistaken for each other. This can be tricky, because you need to be sure you *are* one before you live by the HSP manual, so you do not become too hard on yourself when you notice you can't relate to many of their norms.

Remember from the first chapter that Empaths and HSPs are different, though they might have similar attributes. To better understand this, you need to know more about the differences between these two types, so you do not mistake yourself for an HSP if you are really just an Empath – or vice versa.

Although someone could be both an Empath and an HSP, you should not just assume you are one or the other. It is best to arm yourself with the facts, so you know the right steps to take to overcome the challenges associated with the label to which you belong.

Who is an Empath?

Before deciding which side, you are sticking to, give yourself a fair chance of understanding both concepts. Now that you know quite a lot about them, let's dive more deeply into the attributes of an Empath.

An Empath is someone with the innate ability to feel the emotions around them, from people's to animals' and plants'. They can do this by absorbing energy from others and taking that energy on as their own (like a sponge).

This person is also seen as having certain paranormal skills –like the psychic ability to sense others' emotions and energies. They are very familiar with other's moods, good or bad, and they somehow completely understand and can relate to them without even having experienced them themselves.

Unlike The Highly Sensitive Person, an Empath's nature is not genetic; neither is it influenced by social status, but it is formed from interactions and relationships with others over time. People pick up this skill right from childhood, and it can be developed as time goes on.

An Empath has an unmissable and often unquestionable sense of knowing because they pick up on vibes rather than emotions, which could easily be misread. They know that all humans comprise energy, and the energy you emit goes a long way toward determining the person you are.

Features of an Empath

Besides what you have gathered so far about Empaths, you also need to know the habits and abilities they have and display naturally. Knowing more about how someone is wired will help you clarify any doubts you had about them.

So, to continue this journey, you will need to turn look into and understand the features of an empath, and they might be what you had in mind (or not).

1. Curiosity about Strangers

Empaths are very curious people, even though their probing might not involve asking questions directly, but rather being intentional about trying to pick up energy signals from those around them. They seem to have an insatiable curiosity for others around them because they have kept the childlike interest that many people claim to have "outgrown," even though it is mostly because of society's influence on others. Society has forced us to mind our business.

If someone tells you they have had a bad day, what's your response? For Empaths, they will most likely resist the urge to impose their opinions on why they think the day was bad for you, even though their guess might be closer to the truth than that of anyone else. They will ask questions and be open to listening and learning from the responses given. Also, since Empaths pick up energy waves, they will know the right questions to ask, not to get on your nerves, but to understand your situation better, and help you find solutions to what you are going through.

2. Challenge Differences and Discover Commonalities

Sometimes, individuals use diversity to create unhealthy labels like "nerds" or "radicals" (that drive the cracks of discord deeper into the walls of the society), and this could affect the social nature of man, causing the minority groups to withdraw and agree to the submission.

Empaths tend to question their own biases and prejudices by searching for what they share with people instead of what divides them. Whether it is race, intellectual development, or social standing, Empaths find a way to bridge the gap of diversity, because we are still the *collective* human race.

Despite the type of Empath you are, you just tend to feel others' pains and struggles, put yourself in their place, and you realize the terrible effects of prejudice on their lives and interactions. *(If more individuals were empathic, we would not have a lot of the wars and conflicts we are facing now in the world.)*

A great example is found during the conflicts between Muslims and Hindus in India, leading up to their independence in 1947. Gandhi (an Indian lawyer, anti-colonial nationalist, and political ethicist) believed that empathizing with one's "adversaries" was the first step toward social tolerance. So, he said, "I am a Muslim! And a Hindu, and a Christian, and a Jew."

3. Highly Sensitive

This aspect is the most confusing in terms of differences. Empaths are known to be very sensitive to their environments and the men and women in them. They quickly pick up the slightest changes in both people and places. This has earned them the tag of being "too sensitive," just like HSPs. They are naturally open and are great listeners, but they easily get into bad moods because they absorb the energy around them, turning it into their own. So, their mood and emotions are very dependent on others, which could be very tricky and tiring. Outsiders might not understand and think they need to "toughen up" because "the world is a tough place."

4. Highly Intuitive

Besides being familiar with others' emotions, Empaths are also in touch with their own feelings and instincts. They can rely heavily on their gut feelings to make decisions and use this ability in their interactions with others.

They can tell when something is not just right with a certain place or person. It appears to them in the form of energy signals picked up by their senses - not thought. This comes in very handy when deciding where to stay when visiting a new city, what business risks to take, and where to invest. Their intuition helps them avoid toxic and manipulative people. They also help others (who may not feel things the way they do) by advising in all the areas.

This trait is ideal for professions that need objective analysis or looking beyond the surface like journalism or detective work, and it is common to see Empaths working in these jobs.

5. Absent-Minded

When you are too busy sensing energy all around you, you might look like a lost or confused person to others. So, Empaths are often seen as individuals with poor concentration. For example, an Empath could be in a conversation with you, suddenly switch his attention to something else because he feels a new vibe, and then try to trace the source because it is not coming from you.

Almost always, empathic people are so overwhelmed by the emotions they are channeling that they lose focus. They are influenced by the muddled-up emotions that swarm around them, which often leads them to become fully occupied with these thoughts and emotions.

6. Tidy and Clean

One thing an Empath can't stand is a mess. They already have a lot to deal with, so why add to their emotional weariness? They do not want to catch bad vibes from the litter on the floor, an untidy worktable, or an unmade bed. They would rather be in a space where things are kept neat and tidy, to help them focus and channel their energy on more productive things. They tend to be minimalistic and cherish simple but tidy spaces.

Types of Empaths

Even though people can't seem to agree on how many types of Empaths there are, generally there are six types. Knowing this and understanding each one of them will help to demystify this concept.

1. Emotional Empath

This is one of the most common people who easily pick up on others' emotional energy. The emotional Empath deeply experiences others' feelings in their own emotional body and can even put themselves into other's shoes (both emotionally and physically). They usually get drained from absorbing so many emotions at a time. The amazing thing is that they can do this without even trying to read these emotions, unlike the HSP.

2. Physical/ Medical Emp

This person is more in tune with the body energy that oozes out of people. These Empaths use their skill to figure out what is wrong with somebody, just by sensing it. They could become "healers," using their abilities to help cure other's bodies. A physical Empath can intuitively sense and feel the physical pain of others, and this is rare.

Think of this: A child develops a headache and complains to his mom, who soon gets one, even while trying to help the child get better. The good thing is that the physical empath, most of the time, knows a solution to others' pains or illnesses.

3. Geomantic Empath

This person is also tagged as a "place or environmental empath" Those with this type of empathy find themselves easily familiar with certain environments or places, even if they have no connection there or might have never been there before. You are most likely a geomantic empathy if you notice you are happy or comfortable in certain places for no plain reason.

Besides this, geomantic Empaths can pick up the energy from places, and that could be because of their history. For example, a mountainside could ooze out the feeling of struggle to a geomantic empath, based on the difficulties that others have faced trying to get to its peak. These Empaths are very drawn to the natural world and find it communicates to their subconscious.

4. Plant Empath

This is quite an interesting side to the Empath. A plant Empath can instinctively sense what plants need. If you are a plant empath, you can tell why a plant is not flourishing or which makes the best place to plant seeds, without studying agriculture or having experience with those types of plants.

These individuals find themselves attracted to greens and might even take on an occupation that involves growing or taking care of plants. They also gain a certain satisfaction from sitting beside/under a tree or in a garden and receiving guidance from nature, clearly hearing the plants in their minds.

5. Animal Empath

Like the plant empath, animal Empaths strongly connect to animals. They can be the people we know as dog, cat, or horse whisperers. Those with this ability understand what animals need, and they can also sense their emotions and moods. They feel drawn to these animals and might communicate with them in a way they understand telepathically.

This is why we find that a stranger might calm our pup down when he is having a panic attack, or make him come out of his shy shell after such a long time trying. The chances are that if you are an animal empath, you are already spending a lot of time with animals, and you feel drawn to them, even if they are not yours. You could also make it into a career path because you might as well spend most of your time doing something you love so much.

6. Claircognizant/Intuitive Empath

This is quite like the emotional empath, but the difference is that the Claircognizant Empath can pick up information from simply from being around others. Unlike sensing emotional energies, it takes only one glance at someone else for an intuitive Empath to gain much insight about him or her.

This ability comes in handy when trying to understand someone you just met. People often put up facades to create a pleasant first impression, though claircognizant Empaths can easily see beyond that. It also makes them great counselors and advisers.

Other types of Empaths that have received attention over the years include:

- Telepathic Empaths - reading people's thoughts correctly

- Medium Empaths - connecting to the souls of departed people

- Psychometric Empaths - gaining information about people and things by touching physical objects

- Precognitive Empaths - feeling or experiencing an event before it occurs.

Differences between Empaths and HSPs

There are a lot of correlations between Empaths and HSPs, and it is normal that individuals mix them up. For you to know where you stand, their differences must be highlighted, but remember that you could be both an Empath and an HSP.

1. Their Abilities

While HSPs have a heightened central nervous system, making them different from others, Empaths have paranormal skills like:

> • Psychic abilities - the ability to sense what is hidden from others in the form of energy waves

> • Clairaudience - the ability to hear what is inaudible to the ordinary human ear

> • Clairsentience - the ability to view past, present or future physical or emotional feeling of others using none of the five senses.

This means Empaths are seen as having a form of sixth sense, while the senses of an HSP is sharper.

Let us say two friends were just involved in a heated argument, and an HSP steps into the room. Even though they try to pretend nothing has happened, the HSP will pick up on cues (like body language) to tell that something is wrong. If one or both friends leave the area and an Empath comes in, he would feel the energy of the argument that happened there without seeing either of them. You can now ask yourself which ability you have.

2. High Sensitivity

Basically, all Empaths are highly sensitive, but not all Highly Sensitive Persons are Empaths. Many are empathetic instead, and this differs from being an Empath. Empathetic people need to have interaction with others before they extend empathy toward them, unlike Empaths who can be in tune with others they know nothing about, just by recognizing their energy. As a result, they find themselves absorbing those feelings and emotions.

3. Harnessing Their Gifts

Since Empaths pick up on energy and HSPs notice sensory stimuli, the way they tap into their gifts differ. For the Empaths, they often channel their gifts into something deeper to help people out, because that is their drive. So, we discover that most mediums, psychics, and spiritualists are Empaths. Meanwhile, HSPs learn how to be mindful of their sensitivity to help their interactions with others (relationship or career-wise).

Chapter 4: Health Concerns for the HSP

The journey to discovering the Highly Sensitive Person would not be complete without considering the problems they face. The fact that they have unique abilities does not mean everything just works out fine for them. Do you know how much the HSP trait tends to wear out its bearer and could potentially lead to serious health issues for them? If not, let's get informed right now!

For starters, some who do not yet identify with their trait (and worry that they are abnormal) might take on all sorts of activities and take substances to try to suppress their innate abilities. They are tired of feeling drained all the time. They want to explore the world like others without feeling too scared or overthinking things. They might want to be spontaneous and handle situations better. This could make them turn to caffeine, alcohol, or hard drugs for help.

In turn, these addictions have a more damaging effect on their minds and bodies. But they do not know better, which is why individuals need to be clear about who they are and why they wired in a certain way. This information aims at bridging that gap, but first, you need to be in the know about the health concerns for the typical HSP.

Health Concerns

1. Irritability and Intolerance

Let us begin with what some might see as subtleties, because sometimes it takes a small change to make big things happen. It has been found that they may suffer the sensitivity of environmental stimulants such as food, surroundings - and even chemical substances. These may not be in the form of serious allergies; they can influence their quality of life. Common irritants may be lactose-based foods or even reactions caused by gluten.

Irritable bowel syndrome is not a stranger to them because the central nervous system is not only heightened, the enteric (concerning the gastrointestinal tract) nervous system also picks up the sensory cues. This means that as an HSP, you also feel reactive pains and emotions in your gut. The extra load of feelings you are reacting to and trying to process may just be the reason for your stomach pain or digestive discomfort.

Look at the link between what you eat and discomfort levels, tiredness after you have eaten, or the onset of headaches. These symptoms do not apply to all those who are HSPs and, unless they are aware of how to maximize their high sensitivity, they will not know how to handle their intolerances.

2. Depression

It is hard enough trying to figure out why you are so different. Then having the world take you on a "never-ending" emotional rollercoaster ride can seem nerve-racking. So, it's very common for them to fall into states of depression, on both a short- and long-term basis.

Besides, they are known to absorb the emotions of others through their interactions. It means that most of the time, their moods depend on others, and that is not always good. In a world where there is so much bad news and where people express negative emotions, it makes it hard for them to cope with any added emotions.

Aron says that when depressed, an HSP is more likely to have suicidal thoughts because of how deeply things get to them. They might want to find a way to remove themselves from the constant sadness they go through. This is not a solution, though, and realizing that your trait is a gift could be all you need to snap out of feeling hopeless or flawed.

3. Zinc Deficiency

One of the most common mineral deficiencies, with about two billion people affected, is zinc deficiency. Zinc is an essential nutrient that supports the body's ability to heal and repair, and it handles over 300 enzyme functions in the body.

You can look for signs that tell you whether you are suffering from this deficiency, including hair loss, nail health, and even more significant than that, an impaired immune system and even infertility. In severe cases, this can also lead to heart disease.

Studies have revealed that the older we get, the more likely we are to be zinc deficient. One of the main reasons why HSPs could be zinc deficient is that they are prone to higher stress levels, which drains the body's mineral resources, zinc included. Chronic stress occurs when they do not feel in control of their environment over a long period.

Aside from the mild issues mentioned earlier, zinc deficiency could manifest itself in the form of compromised immunity in them, and this means difficulty recovering from infections and susceptibility to colds and viruses.

Because they are humans first, some could have underlying health issues. Those already battling chronic fatigue, adrenal issues, diabetes, and hormonal imbalance might want to pay closer attention to their zinc levels.

4. Addictions

Although there is no proof they are more likely to turn to addiction than the rest of the general population, many have admitted that they resort to excessive food, alcohol, drugs, and other unhealthy practices whenever they feel constantly overwhelmed. This could be their way of trying to "tone down" their sensitivities or momentarily divert their attention away from their problems, but the gratification these addictions offer is very brief, and the need to continue to use this as a crutch becomes a problem.

This takes a toll on their body and mind and may even open them up to new levels of sensitivity triggered by their addiction. Nurturing a favorable lifestyle that supports your health, especially as an HSP, will prove more useful than succumbing to unhealthy cravings. We'll dig into that a little deeper soon, just hang on.

5. Hair Loss

Do you know that stressing yourself out can lead to hair loss? Do you also know that they are grandmasters of stressing over even the smallest of things? Do you see the correlation there? Okay, enough with the questions – let's move on.

The confession of an HSP:

> "While working my first corporate job, I put my health on the line in a dangerous way. I was so obsessed with climbing the ladder and being the best employee that I completely burned out. I began losing hair, losing sleep at night, and developing severe digestive issues." – Alissa Jablonske.

You need not panic when you start losing hair. Your quest for perfection (and the stress that comes with it) could be the cause of it all. Hair loss can also occur because of unresolved emotions. It's common for some of them to yank at their hair when anxious or scared about something. This has been tagged as trichotillomania, and it is not exclusive to them. If you do this, try to make the conscious effort to stop. Finding alternatives to tug at might be a good quick fix, but talking to someone close or a therapist about your anxiety could help stop the habit altogether. They need not do the listening all the time; talking about what is stressing you out could be a great way to get over it.

6. Headaches

With the way they analyze every piece of information, they could get a headache just thinking about why they have headaches all the time. Thinking through so many things in a short span of time takes its toll on you. You might be thinking, "Isn't that what the brain is there for?" Yes, it is, but even our phones can have "blips" when reaching their memory's elastic limit simply by doing "what they are meant to do."

It is harder for them to screen out emotionally draining information from their thoughts, so it weighs on them. The result of this can be constant headaches and even migraines.

Besides stress and overthinking, those who are sensitive to bright lights, sharp sounds, or funny smells will find these triggers also lead to constant headaches. The solution to this is simple. Stay away from your triggers as much as possible to give your brain its much-needed breathing space.

7. Fatigue

What happens when they absorb all the emotional information from those around them? They are drained, and it is very clear. They are great listeners, but they are not the best at letting hurtful information go.

If someone loses a close member of their family and calls their HSP friend to inform them, they can sense the genuine pain in the response, because it is there. Whether intentional or not, they have been implanted with the same type of grief that the caller has; long after the call, they keep ruminating over the news. This is one of the traits of a good friend, but it can be very tiresome when it happens repeatedly, since bad news never stops happening.

For someone who feels things intensely, both internally and externally, this induces Compassion Fatigue, which has been described as the equivalent of an emotional hangover. When everything gets to you, it affects your ability to process and deal with your emotions and other people's emotions. It simply seems too overwhelming. Not everyone who is sensitive will go through this, but they are bound to feel overwhelmed and physically drained.

What an HSP Can Do about these Health Concerns

There is a solution to every problem, but you first must acknowledge the problem, so you are sure to be able to find the best solution for it. Knowing you are an HSP is the first revelation you need to deal with and the challenges attached to it. The next step is to develop some coping mechanism. As we know by now, they vary based on their other traits, and the ways they manifest their HSP trait differ as well.

When you have ticked all the boxes relevant to you in terms of the features of an HSP, its pros and cons, and the health concerns, you should be able to take the steps that relate to what you are facing and adopt solutions for an optimal lifestyle that promotes good health. Now, we can tackle this head-on.

1. Be Mindful of your Diet

This is a great tip for anyone. Healthy eating helps your energy levels, boosts your immune system, and leaves you feeling fresher and better overall. Eating healthy foods can also reveal any food sensitivities or allergies you didn't even know you had.

Now, this does not necessarily mean you should change your whole diet unless you need to. It means you should be more intentional about your food choices. Have you noticed patterns in the way you eat, the foods you are sensitive to, whether the smell, taste, or texture upsets your system? If yes, then you should avoid those foods that trigger adverse reactions. If not, start paying closer attention to what items of your diet are unhealthy. Chances are – you probably already know these.

Also, reducing your alcohol and caffeine intake can spur positive changes in your mood and anxiety levels you did not think were possible. Long after you think these substances are out of your system, their effects can still be very evident in your mind and body.

Aside from these, be aware of your need for zinc, which can be found in protein-rich food, meat, seafood, and even dairy products. Nuts are also a good source. Lamb and cashew nuts are two of the best sources of zinc. Mushrooms and spinach also make the list, so you can choose these if you are zinc deficient. You will be amazed at how some small modifications to your diet can affect your overall health.

2. Cleanse your Environment

Besides consciously staying away from upsetting stimulants, they can also carry out a form of detox on their homes and workspaces. From personal care products like soap, deodorant, perfumes, and body lotions to cleaning products like bleaches and disinfectants used, there should be a general screening. Since these products are for your use, those that make you uncomfortable or that you react to should be replaced with more natural alternatives.

You will also want your space to be clutter-free as a lot of unnecessary and untidy items could throw you off the cliff if you are already going through emotional distress. Rather, replace these items with more thoughtful and calming ones that resonate with the serenity you need. So, whether it is your sense of smell, sight, or hearing, let your environment identify with your needs, rather than trigger your emotional outbursts. Once you are in control of your immediate environment, your stress levels are bound to reduce, and you are just left with the outside influences to conquer.

3. Embrace Self Care

Being everyone's shoulder to lean on can be tough, and you need to have the right energy to be the adviser and friend, everyone knows you to be. What you need to realize, though, is that it all starts with you. Yes, your emotions are all over the place, and yes, you can't seem to let go of emotions, but how about you use all this information to help yourself instead of hindering yourself? Take your own advice and relax. You will find it works wonders for the mind.

Go out into nature, take a long walk, reflect (not in an overthinking kind of way, but calmly ponder over the important stuff), meditate, write or just do a few breathing exercises (take long breaths, through your nostrils, and exhale through your mouth). When you have done at least one of these things, you will begin to feel the energy return little by little, and that you are ready to take the world on again.

4. Have a Reliable Social Circle

No man is an island, especially not the HSP, so being sure that the people within your circle have got your back is key to overcoming many challenges that you might face as an HSP (including the health-related ones).

They are greatly affected by others' moods and emotions. If you always feel exhausted after hanging out with someone, it is time to reassess your relationship with that person and decide if the relationship is toxic to you as some relationships are even to people who are not HSPs. You can limit your interactions with the person to only outdoor gatherings where you are not alone, so that is not the only energy you are feeding on.

Accept that you cannot have such a tight circle and decide not to tell them things. Speak up when you feel uncomfortable, happy, sad, or angry. Do not silence your emotions as this could lead to a state of depression. Help your friends make thoughtful decisions that will help you by speaking out because not everyone can sense others' emotions through their expressions. Sometimes you need to discuss these things.

Above all else, being one is a gift and a permanent part of your identity as a person. Being aware of this gift and how it's harnessed to create a deliberate standard of living that promotes health and wellbeing will help you check and even avert some of your recurring health concerns. Remember, take care of your mind, and your body will respond accordingly. The same works when you take care of your body because the mind reacts in a positive way.

Chapter 5: Parenting Highly Sensitive Children

If your child has been labeled with any of the following adjectives: shy, highly emotional, highly perceptive, you may be raising a highly sensitive child. It may have been a source of interest or worry for you to see just how "different" your child is from his friends or members of his playgroup, making this chapter of utmost importance to you.

By now, you should understand the certain qualities they display. It becomes an interesting topic for children because these are naturally in their formative stages. A child grows up to become highly sensitive when they are incredibly sensitive to happenings in their environment. To a highly sensitive child, the little things matter. Whether it is how someone eats, or it is the mood or smell or reaction of other children when something happens, a highly sensitive child can note these things.

A question that comes to any parent's mind about their highly sensitive child is if such a thing should incite excitement or worry. On the upside, highly sensitive children have an increased and sharpened sense of awareness. They are often gifted and intellectually sound ones. They can show creativity and a high level of emotions at such an early age. The downside to having highly sensitive children is that such an increase in perception could be a catalyst for a lot of emotional trouble.

Having a highly sensitive child is akin to having a child who displays superpowers. Whether it is then used to save the world or destroy, it depends on the level of care and parenting provided. Having a highly sensitive child is normal, but a rich level of parenting is necessary. In the words of Elaine Amor, "... it is primarily parenting that decides whether the expression of sensitivity will be an advantage or a source of anxiety." Parenting is a deciding factor when it comes to how highly sensitive children turn out to be.

This segment will make you ask questions such as: how do I know whether my child is highly sensitive or not? What can I do? What skills or mechanism can I adopt?

Early detection of HSP in children is important. In this chapter, you will find yourself presented with a useful manual by which you can successfully manage a highly sensitive child.

How Do You Know Your Child Is Highly Sensitive?

This section aims to further strengthen the introductory aspect of this chapter. It is not just enough to know what a highly sensitive child is; it is also important to know how you can *detect* a highly sensitive child. These traits prepare parents or teachers for a very important task. In the end, a highly sensitive child should be dealt with delicately. This can happen when the parent or teacher has been armed with the necessary information, but first, you can take this list as a guide to see whether your child is highly sensitive.

1. Asks a Lot of Questions

In some ways, being sensitive and being inquisitive go hand-in-hand. It is natural for children to be curious, but this does not mean that all children are highly sensitive. At the same time, this trait cannot be taken away from a highly sensitive child. Highly sensitive children have a lot of questions to ask almost all the time. This is because, as we have discussed, they are more susceptible to their environment. Being aware of their environment only leads to a lot of "what ifs" and "how did this come to be?" Highly sensitive children want to know everything, and this is very much visible in HSP children.

2. Emotional

A highly sensitive child is likely to be a lot more emotional for their age than normal and has the tendency to react that way to almost everything. A broken toy could make a highly sensitive child feel miserable for the rest of that day, and even beyond that. They feel drawn to certain pains of other people, animals or things and, as such, reason that they could find a way to solve these problems. To an HSP child, they spend a lot of time worrying about other people's problems, and they will constantly seek how they can solve these problems.

3. Good at Observing People

These children have this great sense in terms of observing their environment. For these sensitive children, they are masters at reading people. They can see the character and traits of others and, if asked, they could give a pinpoint description of what or whom they have observed. To put this to the test, you could just ask your sensitive child to describe your character. You will be amazed at just how much information is at their disposal.

4. Slow to Get Over Failure

The phrase "fail quickly and move on" does not sit so well with highly sensitive children. Highly sensitive children are perfectionists. When they do something, they are very careful to the last detail. So, when a singular mistake is made, a lot of things could go awry. Sensitive children simply want to know why that particular plan failed. They brood over the event and tend to ask multiple questions about why they did not realize that their plan was not going as smoothly as it should. They want to know how the problem can be resolved and, often, this could cause stress and anxiety.

5. Gets Upset Easily

Another common trait you may have noticed in sensitive children: getting upset easily. Sensitive children are just that–sensitive, and because of this, little things can upset them. A resultant factor is that they ruminate over problems for a long time, and if they get upset with you, it could take a while before they will talk about it. And because they are hurt about it, they would rather hold on to it than express things to you, at least until they find a solution on their own terms.

6. A Sensitive Child is Polite

The exterior may be a little tough, but the interior is charming. In sensitive children, you have a group of young, well-mannered people, and they are equally polite within each environment they find themselves in.

7. Bothered by Noisy Places

Peace and quiet are of necessity to sensitive children. They are easily distracted and disturbed by noisy places, and most of the time, if not all the time, they seek quiet places. If your child prefers to stay alone in his room instead of going outside to play with kids of his age group, then he could be considered sensitive.

How Do You Handle A Highly Sensitive Child?

Now you know how to spot a highly sensitive child. The next question should be what to do. This is the critical stage for parents or teachers, and a comprehensive list has been provided below on how to handle highly sensitive children.

1. Accept that Your Child is Highly Sensitive

Before anything else, a parent or teacher must accept the nature of their child. As a parent or teacher, it is normal to be worried about your child's obvious super sensitive nature, but understand two things. First, your child did not ask to be hypersensitive, and second, it is up to you as the parent or teacher and not the child, to tailor this high sensitivity into something positive. Forcing your child to change could be very dangerous, and this could change his behavior in a detrimental way. It is very important then that you see your child as special and not as a misfit. See your child's sensitivity as a *gift.*

2. Always Encourage Your Child When They Showcase Their Positive Traits

We have discussed the upside and downside associated with highly sensitive children. A strategic way to reduce the latter as much as possible is to encourage your child's positive traits. As much as you can, try to let your child see the good in showcasing their positive traits. Focus on your child's strengths. Parenting highly sensitive children includes supporting them, especially when they have done something positive. It becomes your duty than as a parent or teacher to help your child realize these qualities and even help him want to do a lot more positive things.

3. Understand Your Child's Feelings

A sensitive child has a load of high-range emotions flowing through them. Therefore, one of the first steps of a parent or teacher is to understand these feelings. Because of their high level of sensitivity, emotions can get out of hand. One wrong move by a parent is to become oblivious to this point or to ignore it. Instead, learn to accept it and be receptive to it.

4. Seek to Reassure Your Child

Highly sensitive children constantly stay aware of their environment. They know that they differ from other children, and sometimes they see it in others' attitude toward them. A sensitive child is likely to feel rejected by his peers, and as a parent or teacher, you should constantly remind them there is absolutely nothing wrong with being sensitive. Encourage your child through your words and through your actions so they do not feel separated from the outside world.

5. Guide our Child

At this stage in a child's life, they need every bit of guidance they can get. It is not just enough to see or accept that they are sensitive. It is also imperative to provide yourself as a parent or teacher when they are set to make certain choices. Create regular conversations with your child and help them face social situations. Social interaction is likely to be difficult for a sensitive child. Your contribution to your child's development matters. Work together as a team, and gradually; you will see signs of improvement. Do not decide for your child; instead, help the child make the right decisions and praise her to help develop their self-confidence.

6. Be Calm and Patient

Most importantly, as a parent or teacher, understand that patience is a virtue. You are likely to lose it at times with your child because you may have different perspectives about things. This is where you should note that your child is displaying a personality trait. Your child is only doing things the best way they know how.

Subscribe to looking at things from your child's perspective and reaching an agreement with him. Also, understand that things may not work out well if you try to enforce your own beliefs in this situation. Furthermore, if you are too upset to handle your child, seek your partner's help or step away to a quiet place until you can deal with the situation in a sensitive manner.

7. Planning is Key

You already know the personality of your child. It is now up to you to plan ahead so you can handle your highly sensitive child. The first level of planning involves your child. Take your plans through your child and ensure you are both on the same page as to how you can manage their personality. By planning with your child, you can know certain things like what they like and what they do not like, how much social interaction they can cope with, and what kind of activities they enjoy. When you involve your child in such plans, you are halfway there in helping them cope with situations as and when they happen.

8. Prevent your Child from being Bullied

Sensitive children are easier prey for bullies, seemingly because of their personality. A sensitive child does things differently from his peers, and that is enough to make him the subject of attention from bullies. As a parent or teacher, you must protect your child from bullies as much as possible. You cannot be with your child all the time, but you can build your child's confidence. When your child can share their fears with you, their confidence levels grow, and this will go a long way in shielding them from bullying behavior. Continually make your child feel safe and boost his confidence level. And since you cannot be with your child all the time, you can count on your child's established friendships.

Importance of Early Detection of High Sensitivity in Children

Having a highly sensitive child should not be thought of as an obstacle. It is simply a neutral trait. One way a parent or teacher can be in firm control is to be able to detect a highly sensitive child early on – which is why this chapter is very important when dealing with highly sensitive children.

For parents, detecting if your child is highly sensitive saves you precious time from wondering whether you should be worried. Now that you understand what it means to have a highly sensitive child, you can create a suitable environment for your child.

For teachers, favorable learning experiences can be provided for the HSP child. A learning environment can be constructed to match the highly sensitive child's strengths and continually build these traits to make them a better and more capable person.

Chapter 6: Relationship Challenges for a Highly Sensitive Person

Falling in love and being in a relationship carries with it many different shades of emotion, and this is for everyone - whether you are an HSP or a non-HSP. Sometimes, it seems impossible to think of the bursts of happiness you might feel now, and the little drops of sorrow that come right after, which are all part of being in a relationship. In truth, this is a reality for everyone, but overwhelmingly so for a highly sensitive person.

In the earlier chapters, we discussed several features that make them different from others. Whether it is about being intuitive or being highly sensitive or perceiving people's emotions, these characteristics can work out either advantageously or badly when their involved in a relationship.

They are regarded as special people - something that has been justified by the 20% of highly sensitive persons in the world. Statistically, they are already mingling with the other 80% of the world of not-highly sensitives, and relationships between the two are likely to ensue. When one gets involved in a relationship with a non-HSP, it can be likened to two different worlds trying to form a coalition. These are two people with different psychological and emotional peculiarities. Depending on the knowledge depth of both parties, such relationships might succeed or might fail. They have a different view of reality, but this gift or trait might be the very reason that could make them vulnerable in a relationship. And most do not understand the gravity of their traits when they are in a relationship, leading to such relationships crumbling.

When this happens, a popular question that comes up in the mind of an HSP is 'What is wrong with me?' Things become overwhelming for them, and it feels like no matter what is being done, they simply cannot hold on to the relationship.

This point is fueled largely by the lack of understanding of them. Even *they* fail to look at their unique traits and how their sensitivity can change virtually everything.

It is why this book, and particularly this chapter, helps shorten the knowledge gap and look at what exactly can be done with HSPs and relationships.

The Difference Between a Highly Sensitive Person and Non- Highly Sensitive Person

As has been mentioned several times, a highly sensitive person is special, but just how do they differ from a non-highly sensitive person? High sensitivity affects their relationships. The embedded personality traits in both an HSP and a non-HSP are enough to cause challenges in a relationship. Often, the task is to see just how both differ in their personalities.

One critical way of separating the HSP from the non-HSP is looking at the energy level put into the relationship. Although they would rather remain alone because they believe that their traits could be harmful or provoking in a relationship, they fall in love easily due to their personality. They have that virtue of feeling deeply for people, and such emotions can transcend into falling and being in love. Due to the emotional attraction and attention they provide, they are filled with that high energy.

Even if it sounds pleasing to anyone, it is usually the catalyst for the many challenges a couple boasting at least one highly sensitive person will face.

Being one means it is possible to realize that your partner does not agree with many things you believe in. This may not strike you at once, but gradually. Your partner will not appreciate the same things you appreciate. The emotional depth in both parties differs since your partner will not likely view things the same way you do, except for acknowledging that the depth of emotions will be different. When this happens, you may feel disappointed or frustrated, and cracks will appear in the relationship. Subsequently, you may even feel that it is about to crumble. When you and your partner are different emotionally, you begin to demand things they cannot offer. Your partner cannot offer these things because *they do not understand them.*

The problem here is not even about what a partner can or cannot do. The problem lies in them not being able to realize that their partner isn't on the same level as they are. Even though disappointments and misunderstandings are normal in every relationship, they are elements that will continue to occur with them if they do not seek to discover themselves. Part of that is seeing how being a highly sensitive person can affect their relationships.

How Can Being an HSP Affect Your Relationship?

HSPs can make a relationship feel wonderful and, conversely, are also capable of making a relationship feel dangerous. They can affect their relationship either positively or negatively; it all depends on understanding their sensitivity. Although, before you think any safe boundary should be built, first know how being one can affect your relationship both positively and negatively.

1. Attentive

One of the most common traits of these individuals is their observant nature. They are good at studying their environment and the surrounding people. From important things to even the minute details, they leave no stone unturned. This is particularly special in a relationship because by being observant, they can draw out a lot of details about their partner. If an HSP is very good at observing, it means that they are likely to look for abstract things in their partner, like their confidence, inner beauty, or talents. Having an observant person for a partner is likely to boost both parties' confidence in such a relationship. The downside to this high level of observance is the obsessive behavior that comes with it. The observant nature could make you don a judgmental stance, and you may always see faults in your partner. They are likely to take things a bit too seriously just by being observant, and this becomes a worry even for their partners.

2. Compassionate

They are highly compassionate. There seems to be no harm done when they show so much love, care, and support toward their partners' wellbeing, but this deep awareness and empathy shown to partners can become a problem. If they can take too much of their partner's emotions on as their own, it simply means they will experience a similar flow of emotions. It means that if their partner is down or sad, the highly sensitive partner is also down or sad. Relationships supply strong support for emotional balance, and if one person is depressed, the other person should be able to support. This is hard to do for them because if your partner is the constantly moody or anxious type, you will constantly be moody.

3. Conscientious

HSPs are blessed with the gift of being highly sensitive. They can see things from a lot of angles, and they often set high standards for themselves. There is nothing wrong with trying to be better, except that when they fall short of those lofty standards, they primarily shoulder the blame. That nobody is perfect does not seem to resonate well with them. They consider it a monumental failure, and it takes a lot of time to get over it. In the process, intimacy with their partner is lost, and distance hinders the relationship. Part of the high standard for them could be the expectation that a partner should have the same traits as they have. This means they are expecting their partner to be as observant and as caring as they are, which is normal and human. Disappointment sets in when there is no such feeling of reciprocity, and the wrongful notion that your partner does not love you can become difficult to cope with.

4. Caring

There is no such thing as being too caring in a relationship, but for them, one might call it an unintended consequence because they can pick up on every detail and every element that denotes care on the part of their partner due to the traits associated with being a highly sensitive person. In that manner, they can meet even the smallest of needs of their partner, but they often forget to meet their own needs. If you care so much for your partner and neglect your own needs, you gradually become exhausted, and it weighs you down. Being caring MUST extend to caring for yourself as well as others.

5. Moody

The word "mood" encapsulates everything about being in one. There may be no such thing as a constant mood with HSPs; their mood changes like the weather. So, if an HSP is healthy, for instance, they are likely to have a much enjoyable presence around their partner, and the relationship becomes even energy-filled. But they can get irritated or angry around the same partner in double-quick time. This is where certain things being done by the partner can overstimulate them. For instance, if the partner talks a lot or is very active, they might find themselves with a short fuse.

6. Contentedness

There is that danger of a relationship between them and their partner losing its excitement when there is a difference in what they enjoy. They may be okay with simple things – something like watching nature or seeing paintings at an art gallery, and HSPs may stretch themselves to go along with their partner's social likes and dislikes. People have different interests, and when the partner of one does not hold the same interests as their spouse, they may interpret this as a lack of love or caring, placing the relationship under strain. Although it is usual for them to care more about the interests of his/her partner, equal attention should be given to their interests as well.

7. Misunderstood

Their nature has been explored in this book - and specifically in this chapter – so, it is no-brainer to mention that they are misunderstood a lot of the time. They process information so deeply that it often takes longer for them to keep up with a conversation, especially a fast-paced one. When that happens, their partner finds it easy to misunderstand them. A caring partner must slow down the conversation to take account of their need to digest information carefully.

8. Vulnerable

As an HSP, emotions and feelings flood your mind quickly and "thickly." With that heightened sense of emotions, it can be difficult for you to voice needs or desires to your partner without looking like you are overreacting. HSPs tend to speak with strong conviction. What happens? Of course, the relationship can collapse, although an explanation of the condition may help a partner to be more receptive.

9. Forgetting to Include Downtime.

Some romantic relationships end for HSPs because they are too concerned about being a good person in the relationship, failing to create personal moments (or "downtime".) Since a sensitive person is over-stimulated, a moment to self soothe is constantly needed. Being a good partner doesn't always ensure a successful relationship, and it's wise to remember that the depth of the emotions you put forth does not measure your relationship. There are two of you in the relationship, and both of you need downtime.

10. Easily Intimidated

HSPs are likely to find it too stimulating being confronted by their partner. They sometimes find it difficult to deal with the various questions being thrown at them. It becomes a lot worse when their partners read such behavior to mean they are hiding something. Being unable to deal with confrontation might prevent you from being honest, leading to a failed relationship when your partner mistakes it as a lack of intimacy.

Handling Your Relationship, The Right Way

There is a definite need to create safe boundaries for HSPs in romantic relationships. This is because they are vulnerable going into any kind of relationship. With those visible traits, you can become at the center of a lot of faults found in your relationship. And even when it looks like you are not at fault, your partner may be quick to pin the blame on you due to your behavior. Boundaries help you to avoid that.

This is not to say that HSPs should not fall in love or be in a relationship. Everyone can be in a relationship, whether they are sensitive or not. What it means is that they should understand certain aspects of their traits.

The first, and most important, is that you should see yourself as *gifted, (not cursed)*, as a highly sensitive person. It takes a lot of self-doubt away when you live in this reality. Of course, it does not mean they should not go through the process of self-discovery, and it does not mean you should neglect all that has been written in this chapter. It DOES mean that certain boundaries are needed to protect you from harm and the potential of unnecessary arguments.

Another aspect to consider as one, is that not everyone will see things the way you you see them. There are a lot of problems you can solve just by realizing this. Everyone has a different way of viewing things, whether they are sensitive or not, and it means that feelings will also be different. Still, as an HSP, your partner can devote attention to you and making you feel the love you want.

As a sensitive person, keeping your boundaries intact will help you keep a great deal of self-esteem. Self-esteem is what keeps sensitive persons in check while trying to be who they are. They can survive a relationship when they are open-minded about their behavior and attitude, and giving themselves that all-important personal value. If positive parents have brought you up as an HSP, use their example to explain to your partner how your mind works, making them aware of why you need to set boundaries and what you may experience if these are not in place.

Being one can make you have the best of relationships only if you truly understand your sensitivity and share it with your partner.

Chapter 7: Exploring Career Options For The HSP

Everyone spends a lot of their time and energy on their careers. Understandably, bad career choices lead to lots of problems, and we are better off doing something that complements our abilities and natural tendencies. Discovering how well suited your personality and passions are with your potential career choice could save you from regrets and feeling unfulfilled.

As the sensitive souls they are, HSPs must be more deliberate about their career choices, so they don't end up being miserable. Because not all of them are the same, what could be perfect for one might not be a good fit for another. Still, they have many options to choose from because they have a lot to offer. Knowing your strengths and weaknesses make it easier to tell what career choices are best for you. Just make sure you can be your true self when working, so work does not become another stress trigger.

Whether it is tapping into your creativity or analytical skills, your career should bring out the confidence in you. For those who tend to overthink, constantly feeling incompetent at work will hinder their productivity.

Factors To Consider When Exploring Career Options

Based on this, some factors to consider when choosing a career path include:

1. Passion

This works for everyone because we need to be emotionally invested in whatever we are doing to feel its impact. There should always be a certain amount of drive when you choose the work you want to do, whether you are working from home or outside of it. Working should not just be about making money, but adding value and creating lasting memories.

As an HSP, this is where you might have to do some soul-searching. What do you find yourself doing that you love and that you will not mind doing long-term? Where do you find your abilities thriving the most? What sort of work gives you purpose? The truth is, no matter what your choice is, there will be moments when work seems overwhelming, but if you are passionate about your job, that passion will motivate you to overcome problems.

Often, we see successful people change careers because they just cannot let their passions go. It is never too late to chase your passion, but the earlier you do, the better. Your career should have meaning and align with your values so you feel fulfilled at the end of it all.

2. Time

On average, a full-time employee in America works 38.6 hours per week and 1,768 hours in a year. That's a lot of time, no matter how you look at it. So, it would be best if you made sure that each hour is worth it. Are you currently working? If yes, are you fulfilled with where you are and do you think you're fulfilling your purpose?

When deciding on a career, thinking about the bigger picture may seem difficult, but it is necessary. How many hours are you able to work in a week? What times of the day are you most productive? How long do you intend to stay in your job? Do you have plans to set up an enterprise? The answers to these questions will determine how well you thrive in your chosen career.

Besides these tips, those who prefer being in their own space and taking their time in decision-making are better off working as freelancers or business owners than typical 9 to 5 employees.

3. Ability

Aside from being driven and having all the time in the world for a particular job or career, you need to be sure that you can do the job. It is not unusual to see that things we thought were easy to turn out to be a lot harder. One fact that helps clarify this is that knowledge, skills, and abilities differ, but all are needed to thrive in our various careers. "How can I tell the difference?" you may ask. Well, this question ought to do the trick:

"Do you know how to cut hair?" This may seem like a funny question. Your answer to this question is probably yes. I asked how to cut hair; you might have said, "using scissors" or even go further to explain how to cut it in sections for evenness. That's basic knowledge for you. If you are asked to prove your skills well . . . now, we'll know just *how well* you cut hair. Someone who might not necessarily be a hairdresser, but who knows how to produce good results regardless, has the inherent ability (otherwise known as talent). Someone who shows expertise and leaves a desirable result is skilled at cutting hair. That's why you do not just go to anyone to get your haircut. It is the same for a career path.

Sometimes, your ability and skills may not be on the same level. You might have a knack for writing. Let's say you won every essay competition in high school, but does that mean you have the skill to own a column in a Business Journal? No, it does not, but thankfully, skills are always ready to be picked up and learned, and your determination and effort will make all the difference.

We never stop learning, so besides your innate abilities - being empathic, thoughtful, meticulous, and artistically inclined, update your skill reserve to remain relevant and able to do the job, without upsetting you all the time. This you will find to be a great coping mechanism because we all know how everything can be so different for them.

Now that we have that part out of the way, you might already even have great ideas for what your next job should be! If not, put your mind at ease as we discover a few of the career choices that could be great for HSPs. Remember, though, that it all boils down to you. Don't choose a career path just because someone says it is right for you. You need to make sure that it aligns with your personality, pace, abilities, and vision.

Let's get to it then, shall we? What are the best career options for HSFs, and why are they great choices?

Career Options for The HSP

Healthcare

Whether it is that meticulous doctor who does not stop until a solution to an anomaly is found, or the most caring nurse, who forms a bond with every patient, many thrive in healthcare. The first thing that would drive a person to consider medicine or healthcare as a career (besides the desire to help people and save lives) is curiosity. Remember, they want to know more about every piece of information they get to make everyday decisions. How much more when it involves lives? These fields also align with other HSP strengths like empathy, compassion, and intuitive knowledge of others' feelings.

Besides being a doctor or nurse, there are other aspects of healthcare HSPs are suited to:

- Psychotherapy - using Psychology to solve mental health issues

- Physical therapy - treating diseases and injuries through physical methods like massage, heat treatment, and exercise, rather than drugs or surgery

- Dietetics - using the right diet to promote good health and nutrition

- Personal Coaching - following patients on the journey to engaging in self-care and developing long-term health goals.

There will certainly be a lot of emotions from others to deal with, but many are naturally drawn to these fields. As long as there is passion, other variables are bearable. Besides, you will experience people's emotions anyway, so you might as well go through it when working on something you love and find fulfilling.

Creative Industry

While everyone wants to see himself or herself as creative, this trait is more evident in certain people, and they make up a percentage of those individuals. We are witnesses to creativity every day; from the movies we watch to the ads we see, songs we listen to, and even books we read. These are all products of one creative process or another. While a few creatives are at the forefront, like fashion designers, musicians, fine artists, actors, and authors, others put in work behind the scenes to either support the creatives or add aesthetics to their work, like editors, photographers, directors, social media managers and graphic designers. They are all people who put their artistic talents to work as a day job.

With the way they notice various subtleties, they put more effort into ensuring that their output is great and free from any mistakes. This is rewarding and is a very sought-after ability in the creative industry because besides talent, attention to detail is important to be the best.

Besides this, creative jobs are easily done freelance style, and even remotely at times, so this affords them time and space to harness the creativity within and do all the information unpacking before turning in their work. Is that not just awesome? Being a creative professional is also a way to build professional experiences, network, and build yourself as an artist, if you plan to venture out on your own.

Academia

Here, the insight and thoughtfulness of an HSP is explored because careers in academia revolve around counseling, teaching, lecturing, researching, and analyzing. According to an article in Forbes Magazine, they have very active minds. The part of the brain related to attention is enhanced, making it easier for them to pay attention to detail, planning, making the right decisions, and using intuition. Hence, they tend to thrive in academics.

Although academia is a very competitive field, it gives room for them to tap into their strengths. Even as students, they tend to be the ones who keep the teacher back for a few minutes after class, to further explain a concept to them because they would like to know more about the new topic they just discovered.

Since research and learning never end in this field, the hunger for understanding will continue to be fed. Also, sensing others' hidden emotions, an HSP lecturer will easily pick up cues when students are not following a particular lecture and can change techniques to gain their attention. This ability also comes in handy for school counselors. Students will be more open to someone who can relate to what they are going through without asking them too many questions or seeming judgmental.

Another thing with academics is that you get to specialize, so you're not all over the place. You're just teaching people about what you already have a passion for, and you get to make an impact and build meaningful memories while doing your job. We often hear people's success stories built on how remarkable academics made the ride to the top smoother for their students. This is simply an academic's delight, besides all the other perks. How much more could one expect for an HSP who cherishes positive emotions so much?

Self-Employment

As much as making an impact in other people's organizations can be fulfilling, running your own business success could be all the reassurance you need to know that you are valuable to society. You may also feel your ideas and efforts are too precious to spend building another person's empire, so you would rather dedicate all that time and energy to your own endeavor. Whichever way you look at it, running your own business can be a breath of fresh air.

However, not everyone is up to this task because business ownership comes with its challenges. Do not fear, though, if you have a clear vision and can pass it on to your employees and environment, as those challenges will be easier to breeze through.

Another advantage is that you get to set up your workspace to your taste, from the décor to the scents and every other detail you find important. Also, your schedule is not left out of the plan. You know what times of the day are most productive for you, so you can build a schedule around them, and spend the rest of the day doing other meaningful things, and resting (which is very important).

You also are better working with your team because you will be more considerate of their plights than others would be. You also care for their wellbeing, because you know that it aids productivity, and everything goes smoothly when you are in the best frame of mind.

Remember that stress comes from feeling like you've lost control of your environment. This means owning your business will reduce your stress levels.

Non-Profit Work

Working for non-profit organizations might not be many people's dream job, but it could be very satisfying for someone who would like to add value and make an impact in the grand scheme of things. It's all about the scope, really. If you're passionate about a cause and you know there are organizations where you can lend your support not just by donating, but also offering your services, why wouldn't you? But just like every other profession, this comes with its flip side. Working or non-profit organizations could be as stressful, or even more difficult, than private-sector work. So, choose carefully.

They often find that non-profit professions fit them well. These include administrative work, grant research work, helping with fundraising, and even marketing and direction of projects that help others (depending on how demanding the work is).

Stay within the safe levels of your capabilities. Also, don't let the level of pay weigh heavily on you. You can always pick up remote freelance jobs based on your skills and make extra money.

IT Sector

With the world heavily dependent on technology, reliable people are needed in the Information Technology space to make sure that websites aren't crashing, apps are functioning well, hackers aren't having a field day, and overall, that the IT world keeps getting better. Understanding the dynamics of computer software and hardware, the Internet, and how they can be used for everyone's good, then infusing it into solution-based work requires creativity, precision, and the right amount of intuition, are all parts of their wheelhouse.

Whether it is coding, programming, hardware installation, or web development, their attention to detail will come in handy. They will also need little or no supervision because they are result-oriented people and need not be supervised to be productive. Their thought patterns will also be needed when drawing up algorithms to be used, and in the case of any issue, they do all they can to resolve it.

Besides these advantages, IT workspaces are usually less tense than the typical private sector offices, and the professionals can do their jobs without getting distracted. Although your colleagues' attitude also goes a long way toward determining how your job will go for you, be open to the opportunity to meet people, learn from them, and network.

There's a lot of remote work in the IT sector, so you could work from the comfort of your own space, but don't be afraid to work with other people. If there's one thing we can't stay away from in this world, it is people. So, you might as well stand and face your fears, knowing you have value to bring to the table, and nobody can make you feel any less valuable. Besides, working with individuals with similar interests will enhance your knowledge and understanding.

Reiterating what was earlier mentioned, these are just guides, not a blueprint. The decision is always yours. If you have a passion outside of these choices from which you can make a career (after weighing up the pros and cons, as you typically do), take the steps to secure the job of your preference.

Chapter 8: Pets and HSPs

It might seem confusing initially, but two things that go together are HSPs and pets. That is because there is a connection between them and their pets. In the earlier chapters, you will have come across hints of why they should have pets; we'll dive deeper in this chapter.

Research has shown that pets are highly beneficial to humans, but their impact on HSPs is overwhelming. Dr. Elaine Aron, the author of The Highly Sensitive Child, explains that HSPs could enjoy having pets by their side because of their empathy and emotional responsiveness. Speaking of HSPs (in children), she says, "Being sensitive to the animals surrounding us can benefit them - not just their physical wellbeing but their mental health, too. And it helps us by connecting us with individuals who are sensitive, subtle, discriminating, and loyal to their friends."

Having pets can be a wonderful experience, but it is an especially important experience for them - especially children. Since highly sensitive children are at their developing stage, getting them a pet is likely to do them a world of good. There is that special connection between sensitive children and pets, and through these pets, sensitive children learn a lot of things that will help their emotional and behavioral development. These sensitive children can have their 'companion animal,' and interestingly, these pets are also able to connect with human feelings. For instance, research has shown that horses can read human facial expressions, and they can also remember people's emotional states and adapt their behavior to them. But dogs produce the same feelings of human love and the same brain hormones when you look into their eyes.

It is only logical for them to have a pet at a young age because of how early these personality traits appear and because of the super emotions wired into their brains. Sensitive children especially learn a lot of things about pets. They even learn about grief when these pets die, and while it is usually a painful moment, it helps build their emotional behaviors and responses, preparing them for the world.

This chapter digs deeper into the world of HSPs and pets, especially why losing a pet is a big deal for them and how they can deal with pet loss.

What are the Best Animals for Highly Sensitive Persons?

They find it difficult to move in tune with the rest of the world because of their personality traits. This is where an animal becomes their best friend. Research proves that dogs can reduce an individual's stress and lower their blood pressure. Specifically, breeds like the Chihuahua, Yorkshire terrier and the Cavalier King Charles Spaniel are the best animals for HSPs.

One might wonder what brings about this strong connection or attraction with them and animals. The logic is best understood by those who can find solace in cute and loving animals.

Why is the Death of a Pet so Difficult for HSP?

Naturally, losing a beloved pet is a big deal for everyone, whether they are sensitive or not. Pets are highly important and cherished by their owners. If it is so important for the ordinary person, you can imagine what it will be like for the sensitive person. Many animals supply the emotional cues a sensitive person is accustomed to, such as love, acceptance, and support. And the best part about it is that they are free from the problems of trying to explain themselves. This is where pets become important to them.

With an ordinary person who could be or could not be sensitive, you are likely to have issues based on your personality traits too great to deny a conversation (see earlier chapters). But, since a dog does not talk, you can move about freely and not get to worry about your actions. HSPs know that animals can be easy to understand and are even emotionally stable compared to humans. Therefore, when they lose a pet, their world stops for a length of time until they gradually get themselves together and move on.

For highly sensitive children, they suffer a great deal of pain when they lose their pets. In a world where being sensitive could make you look like the weirdest person around, sensitive children seek solace in these pets. So, when it happens (the loss of a pet), they become depressed and could have a serious emotional breakdown. Having a pet is therapeutic for most HSPs.

How Can Highly Sensitive Persons Deal with Pet Loss?

Losing a pet is of great concern to them. Since they are deep thinkers, they process things differently and more often find it difficult to get over a loved one - or a beloved pet. They feel these losses a little more deeply than any other person would.

And while it comes as a big deal to them, there are still ways they can cope with losing their pets.

1. Feel the Loss

When you lose a pet, you feel like the world has knocked you over. It might be okay, then, to remain on the ground. It is natural to get overwhelmed by your feelings, and you should allow yourself to let out your emotions.

Grief happens differently to different people, and it also occurs in stages. Many experience grief in different stages too, and they could become hypersensitive. Being hypersensitive is not exactly something that should be associated with HSPs, as even without losing a pet, they face several daily challenges. When the moment of grief comes, your best bet is not to hurry or force it as that could bring another bout of emotional problems.

Don't try too hard to let it go. You might not be ready to move on, just like in a broken relationship. You don't quickly move ahead to another or deny you are hurt after the one you thought was your soul mate cheated and dumped you. Cry it out, feel the loss, and in that might come your strength to move on beyond losing your pet gradually.

2. Let People Help You with Your Grief

It is already known that they isolate themselves, even when in grief. It seems uncomfortable to say, but a sensitive person cannot handle grief all alone. This is the part where you should reach out to a close family member or a friend. It is natural to feel that nobody will want to take up the role of associating with you due to your personality trait, but you might be surprised to discover there *are* people out there waiting to help you in your time of need.

The door is to be opened by you. Accept graciously when your family and friends offer to help. It's okay to believe you can heal all by yourself with time, but you may underestimate the positive impact of grieving with loved ones.

It's as though you have a shoulder to lean on, a partner to share the sadness with. Your pet cannot come back to you, but the journey ahead requires your attention and commitment. Loved ones are better at helping you understand the benefits of moving on; it can be hard convincing yourself of a better life ahead without your pet.

3. Engage in Activities

It has always been prescribed to engage in healthy activities when faced with grief. This is a great technique in shifting focus from the pain of losing a pet or anyone dear. There are several activities to be done to get your mind away, if only temporarily, from your current mood. You can hang out with your friends and family, or even hold group discussions with people who may have also lost their pets and who have gone through what you are facing. You can also write about your feelings. A good way to escaping grief is documenting your thoughts in a poem, prose, or an essay. This is something you can do during your solitary time.

You can also honor your pet by donating to any animal affiliated charity organization. That's one great way to feel relieved from the grief, knowing you have contributed a great deal to the honor of your dear pet. It's human to feel comforted by this act and practically shows how much you loved the lost pet.

4. Get Help

Previously discussed scenarios might represent the basic experiences of losing a pet. For HSPs, losing a pet might be too great to bear. It could take a lot more than just a friendly comfort to get over this grief, and if not careful, serious psychological complications could occur. Being sensitive might mean it could be too much trouble or too difficult to open up to your loved ones. At this point you need to seek attention before things get even more complicated.

It's important to understand that in this situation—you are your own savior. Pretense will not help, neither will closing the door to loved ones either. You have the key to getting better and seeking help is an important part of it.

As an HSP, it's okay not to disturb or make others inconvenienced with your demands or needs. A part of you tells you to hold on and get better all by yourself, and not to let anyone in on what you are feeling, but you may not find the wholeness to heal and get yourself to forge ahead alone. This recovery aspect is where family and friends can make remarkable contributions and get you back on your feet.

Reach out to friends and family around you when you feel exceedingly overwhelmed and a sense that the impact of your pet's loss or any other uncontrollable misfortune is becoming alarming. As much as you are used to finding a perfect solution within yourself, learn to call on trusted family or friends whenever you sense an unusually overwhelming feeling of sadness.

Chapter 9: Nature's Rewards For The HSP

For being a Highly Sensitive Person, what does *nature* have in store for you? Well, it may seem like *compensation* of a sort. It might also seem like the leverage you have as a highly sensitive person. While see in both perspectives, it should be tilted more toward the latter. As an HSP, your feelings can sometimes get overwhelming, and they get you to elicit responses and reactions much faster than those who are non-HSPS. There is a higher ability to respond to stimuli. Information is interpreted differently, at a different pace, and with a different reaction than non-HSPs. There is also a great inclination toward nature and things that bring peace, serenity, and that state of mind you, as a hypersensitive person, enjoy being in (out of the constant whirlwind in your mind that brings an uproar of emotions).

Nature is a very great source of serenity, and serenity is one big thing that HSPs need occasionally. Consider the scenario of a hypersensitive female; her agile nervous system's constant activity and ever-spinning mind takes information and transforms it into different boxes. She will dissect things in her mind. The fan's loud rumble will suddenly irritate her while the slow but consistent and rhythmic sound of drops from the sink enters her mind. The conflict of thoughts and emotions joined by the cacophony of these stimuli – combined with the sudden thought of not washing an item she had planned to wash last week and then the thought of the uncompleted interpretation of a page from a novel she read last night . . . it's too much information for any human being to process all at once. You can relate to the weight of it all landing on one's brain. You can just visualize how conflicting that must be. In that case, taking a walk outside and enjoying the evening breeze, for instance, or going to a forest can help relieve you of all the pent-up tension you feel. Having experienced such a situation or scenario, you must have at one point, or the other chosen to take a walk outside, to get fresh air and just calm your mind. Perhaps you were unaware of how much going outdoors could help you, yet you felt pulled toward nature. Now, you understand your relationship with nature and how nature has such a great gift in store for you. This is a way for these people to feel in control when thoughts get to be too much for them.

There is an overwhelming drive to interpret and understand issues more intensely than others do, to observe and take in details, and connect on a much deeper and more intimate level. This points undoubtedly to their having a deep and intimate connection with people and things they come in contact with and even more with nature because it has such a natural and quiet aura. Nature rewards them with serenity, a warm embrace and stress and anxiety relief, and being a delight for the ever-agile nervous system and senses.

As you got a glimpse of this chapter's title, did you also think of nature rewarding the HSP as giving them certain leverages over non-HSPs? It's all linked and connected. Nature not only rewards them by giving them the benefit of a cool walk outdoors; they have also benefitted from the generous hands of nature because she has gifted them with the ability to use their senses in a positive way.

Further, they can perceive nature, connect with it, and create so much positivity from what it offers. Those with a highly a sensitive nature have recounted countlessly how they loved (as children) and still love (as adults) to be around nature and bask in natural elements and how incredible it made them feel. It's the way they are wired. If you or any HSP you know have not discovered the wonders that abound in nature, I hope you have now and will get that connection—that peace, and that calm.

What are Nature's Rewards?

1. Nature Further Excites – Yet Calms the Nervous System: As a highly sensitive person, there's a constant need to calm your nerves, to get away from triggers, and experience a blast of peace yet get adventure while on that peaceful trip. What do you think can give such a feeling? Only nature does it. Green environments (the green feel) have been proven to lift people's moods and take them on a journey away from chaos, conflict, and unsettling situations. It brings about a lot of calm and different doses and shades of nature's beauty. Naturally, there are environments that boost your mood, environments with exciting shapes and colors (for instance) – or that inspire the person enjoying that scene. The emphasis is extended with them. Therefore, nature brings an exciting feeling with a particular kind of peace attached to the experience.

2. Ignites Creativity (art, writing, or painting): The sensitive nature of them creates such a structure that prompts creativity in every form, mostly as a means of expression, and as an outlet to let out the overwhelming emotions. Such leverage! To complete the equation, nature comes along and makes it all more effective. The elements of nature – the trees, leaves, rain, greenery, the breeze, the animals – and every part of nature are inspiring. Just being in a natural environment has been proven to be very inspiring. Because of their connectedness to his or her environment, it is normal there is an urge to create, invent, and make something out of what they have in front of them. Seeing the blast of nature all around can inspire and ignite the desire to express (through drawings, paintings, writings, or illustrations) the beauty of nature, what it means to the individual, and what it stands for. Nature inspires them a lot to imagine, create, and produce awesome and striking works. It gets them into a deeper and more intimate sense of connectivity and reasoning that results in creating creative output. Aside from that aspect of igniting creativity from observing nature, nature, in turn, ignites creativity in the sense that during an overflow of emotions in them. Nature stands as an outlet to welcome, embrace and encourage them to express him or herself through creativity, not necessarily by observing this time around, but by just being in that natural environment of calm, peace and beauty and away from chaos.

3. Acts as a Stress Relief: The aura of a natural environment automatically gives off the feeling of relief or a soothing feeling. Nature can alleviate a tough day at work - a continuous row of chaotic events, a busy schedule, a tough deadline, a series of tasks, so much noise on your way back from work, tough calls, and the constant chaos that goes with daily life. The go-to for relaxation and unburdening of stress will always be found in nature. Being in a natural environment, being around nature, and viewing nature reduces stress, anxiety, anger, and fear that could have you filled up with pent up energy.

Health experts have confirmed that individuals get more acquainted with the natural environment, especially in times of distress, fear, anger, or sorrow. Being in nature has been proven to reduce blood pressure, reduce stress levels, and even regulate the heart rate. Nature helps us to deal with pain and sorrow because, as humans, we are prone to get absorbed with the natural environment and find a distraction in it as it draws one into its simplicity. Isn't it beautiful how we are naturally wired to be engrossed with nature and, of course, how nature chooses to reward us (especially the HSP)?

4. Alarm: Being sensitive means you can notice, see, watch, and suspect. This topic does not necessarily fall under nature as an entity, but nature used to clear the mind. Seeing how we are naturally made to be sensitive is a kind of leverage. Because of the sharp, deep, and quick reaction to both internal and external stimuli, HSPs an easily sense something going wrong. (both external and internal). They feel it even before anyone else does and can thus escape from risky situations, inform themselves and other people of danger ahead and act quickly! Being highly sensitive must be nature's gift to the human element of intuition. Don't you think?

Tips to Enjoy Nature's Rewards Even More as an HSP

1. Immerse Yourself in the Embrace of Nature: To get the best of your "nature tour," you actively need to use your sensitivity. Believe that you are present in the moment and make a deliberate effort to make the best of it. It's your nature to take in the scenery and everything that comes with it, but it is of more benefit to you when you choose to be present in the moment. Inhale and exhale deeply, note details, and take in the scenery. Notice how the raindrops fall to the earth, how the animals protect their loved ones, how they eat, how they look, and how the sun rises or sets. The clouds positioned in the sky are worthy of note as these are ever changing. Notice how the breeze blows your hair and calms your mind. The trees move in rhythm to the wind. Just observe the details, as you'd normally do, trying much not to overthink or over process or even over-calculate in order not to ruin the moment. Nature heals, so allow it to heal. Nature soothes, so allow it to soothe you.

2. Remind Yourself of the Main Goal: Your goal is calm, peace, and serenity. Nature helps you get rid of anxiety, pain, fear, anger, and helps you gain peace and serenity. To get the best out of nature, you constantly need to remind yourself of why you are out there in the first place, especially when your mind keeps drifting. You need to make a conscious and subconscious effort to help yourself feel present in the moment, away from the myriad of thoughts and complexities that might your life. Basking in nature is supposed to help distract you from your pains, worries, fears, anxieties, and calm you down. To help you take in the scenery, be in the moment and use your senses to feel the environment's welcome. It would be best if you didn't ruin the moment by allowing unpleasant thoughts to get in the way (only where you need to think things out rationally, and you need nature's embrace to help you as you do that.) To enjoy nature's benefits better, be intentional about enjoying it.

Forest Bathing for HSPs

Forest Bathing is a Japanese art considered as a natural therapy. It is called "shinrin yoku," and it signifies "bathing in the forest." The art implies taking in the forest atmosphere with your senses and or bathing in the forest atmosphere. Quite a few scientists have researched further into the benefits that abound in nature and, specifically, in forest bathing. It has been found that connection with nature, particularly the forest elements (in this case), bridges the gap between man and nature, mostly caused by being indoors and glued to technological tools. A forest bath will help unplug you from toxic environments, technological grip, and the complexities of your daily life. It connects you with the intricacies of nature and allows you to use all your senses (sight, hearing, taste, touch, and smell) to relate to and connect with nature and, in turn, get a relaxing feeling. You can imagine how much more effective it will be for you as a hypersensitive person.

A study by the Environmental Protection Agency revealed that the average American spends 93% of his or her time indoors. This is because people are unavoidably exposed to technological devices (television, mobile phones, tablets, MacBook, laptops, and other electronic gadgets), which has drastically deprived many people of access to nature and its benefits. It has also been found that to make up for this loss of nature's gifts; one need not devote an enormous amount of time to nature. For instance, to forest bathe, an average of two hours is enough time to get the effect needed. Forest bathing provides a bundle of gifts, yet again! To get the best of this forest-bathing gift, all you must do is to make use of all your senses. Take in the atmosphere, smell the air, taste the atmosphere, touch the trees, feel the roughness of the bark, listen to the birds chirping and singing, watch how the leaves wave at you; leave your technological devices at home and let your mind and body do the work of directing you. Roam, breathe, feel, touch, smell, and see how much you have savored serenity and the beauty of nature. After the first try, you will always want to go back for more.

Chapter 10: Self Care Tips for the HSP

They have been given many synonyms (some right, some wrong, a few applicable, and many not so applicable). Among the synonyms attributed to them has sensory processing sensitivity, hypersensitivity, introversion, shyness or high sensitivity, etc. It is important to note that introversion and shyness share common characteristics, but are different. Having noted this and understood a hypersensitive person's characteristics, what are the self-care tips you need to thrive and make the best use of your sensitivities? Read on to learn more.

1. Set Safe Boundaries: As a sensitive person, you need to realize there are boundaries that you must create and support to stay healthy, stay sane, and thrive. Forcing yourselves into relationships could be a huge health risk. How? Letting too many people into your life may not be the problem, but letting too many unnecessary people into your life, as a hypersensitive person, is a big problem. You feel emotions much deeper than non-HSPs and allowing too many people who don't understand or even care to understand how you are wired will put you at great risk of being hurt. Establishing friendships with people who don't care about you creates risks of being betrayed and hurt. Forcing relationships may tend to end with someone who does not care about you, understand you, or even want to be with you, setting you up for needless pain. It could make you feel that being sensitive is a negative thing that sets your relationships up for failure. Take care of yourself and give yourself space to thrive, the opportunity to grow spiritually, and be happy; this is carried out - partly - by setting safe boundaries and not letting just anyone and everybody in.

2. Be Open About How You Feel: When you have rid yourself of unnecessary elements and people around you, you'll feel that breath of fresh air, of being free, and of ridding yourself of toxic people and/or situations. When you feel this way, you can then invest in relationships that mean so much to you and the parties in the relationship. Healthy relationships with people are very important because it helps you grow, lifts you and helps you share your burdens, find support, comfort, encouragement, and even validation. When you can then differentiate valuable relationships from those that are not valuable, you learn to be more open in your relationships. This means being open about what you feel, about what you do not like, about what you love, and what you want. You can build confidence in yourself and deal less unnecessary burdens. Being open about what you are feeling strengthens your relationships more and prevents people from taking advantage of you.

3. Learn to Say No: To thrive, must to learn to say "No" to people and situations that threaten your peace, happiness, health, and self-esteem. The hypersensitive person has a very high likelihood of getting exhausted, frustrated, annoyed, sad, or stressed after a host of draining tasks or situations, manifesting physically, emotionally, or mentally. You know this. So, when situations arise that require you to compromise your peace of mind, happiness, rest, mental health, physical health, emotions, or rules, always examine if it's worth it before jumping in and volunteering. It's understandable how you are wired to care, feel guilty for not being able to help, or say yes, but "no" is an acceptable decision – and one you must learn to comfortably make.

For instance, you have a booked-up day with tasks you must attend to, By the end of the hot, exhausting day, you are headed home to get rest and feel better. A colleague at work approaches you, seeking your help with a particular assignment. You know that your head is spinning and that you are exhausted. Meanwhile, the task can wait. You also know that you could assist with it even if it wasn't at that exact moment, but because of the fear of saying "no" you help with the task and end up drained.

Perhaps you need to study for a test coming on the next day. While studying, your friend comes along and invites you to a party happening that night. First, you know you must study for your test, and second, you know that parties stress you out. knew there was a test you had to attend to the next day and needed to study to prepare for it. Second, you know that going to parties is stressful for you, yet your friend insists that you come along to the party. What do you do?

It's hard for you to refuse your friend's invitation, even if you have the upcoming test a good reason for not going. You need to learn to prioritize and be disciplined. Bring yourself to understand that you cannot always please everybody. The problem with this is that you'll be displeasing yourself a lot of times too. So, to thrive, you need to learn to say no!

4. Relax: It is a no-brainer to mention at this point that rest is very important, but an emphasis is necessary. Relaxing is a huge part of self-care. It helps you release pent-up tension, helps you recharge your batteries, and assists in helping you feel good and see life through better, cleaner lenses – breathing easier! Today, tomorrow, whenever—you need to learn to RELAX!

5. Spend Time with Loved Ones: It has been scientifically proven that spending time with people you love lifts your mood, boosts your mental health, helps you get rid of loneliness, and improves your self-esteem. It also gives you a better outlook on life overall. It's an essential part of self-care to try as much as possible to be around people who boost your mood and make you happy. These are people who you have an instant connection and bond with, who you have a good time with, and, of course, people who make you feel loved, appreciated, and valued.

6. Walks in Nature: Just as it has been explained in the earlier chapter, nature is a very good mood-booster and health-preserving activity. Take walks outside, enjoy the breeze, go forest-bathing, listen to the insects and birds, go to the beach, hang out at the park (if you are comfortable with it). Go outdoors and let the sun smile on you. Walks in nature are not only limited to the daytime; nature supplies gifts at night, as well. Twinkling stars provide star-gazers with benefits like forest bathing, such as reducing blood pressure levels, stress levels and helping to get rid of anger, anxiety, or pain. Isn't it magical, sitting at night and simply watching the stars shine? Focusing deliberately on becoming attuned to night nature is a great relaxation idea.

7. Find a Match: You need to be with people that are a suitable match. Saddling up with people who don't "get" you and can't relate to your feelings shouldn't even be an option. Let the toxic ones go, forging ahead to be with supportive, fun ones who help you thrive. This way, you won't have to worry so much about what you let out (anger, exhaustion, sadness, frustration, inferiority complex). Relating with people who care about you boosts healthy growth, helping you cope better because these people understand your needs, wants, emotions, dos, and don'ts. Don't invest in toxic, unhelpful, negative people!

8. Embrace the Little Things: Little things are often ignored and pushed aside, considered not to be part of the "big picture." Sometimes, those small things accumulate to become the most important in your life. Reinforcing an earlier point about relaxation, create an established alone time to recharge (as this helps you function better and feel refreshed). Doing hobbies, immersing yourself in beautiful moments, taking time out to have fun, hanging out with friends and family, and doing what you love is good for you. Being with people who care about you, strengthening bonds, and changing your home or room's feel to make it more exciting – or even more calming - can help. Getting adequate sleep and exercising are all little activities you just need to find time for. They are a huge part of self-care, deliberately accepting and embracing yourself, feelings, flaws, wins and losses, and recognizing how they have made you grow. Deliberately reflecting and showing gratitude for growth goes a long way toward making you thrive and even do better.

9. Allow Vulnerability: Acknowledging you are sensitive makes you deal with it better and make the best use of it. Allowing for vulnerabilities implies that you are not trying to hide or deny your sensitivity. Rather, you are embracing it. It's been discovered that people who open up about their feelings and even inadequacies tend to be able to handle life better than those who do not. Allowing your vulnerability means giving yourself a voice, speaking up, showing you are human, and it's a great rule to live by. It gives you a chance to discover new experiences, new things about yourself that you have been hiding within you. It allows your partner or friends who you open up to understand you better and help you sail through hard times. It's healthier to acknowledge yourself and all that you come with (strengths and weaknesses) because it helps you move past your phases of darkness, tiredness, weakness, and even pain. It is a part of the self-care tips for them in this list because it is a great way to exercise self-care. Having made the point about being vulnerable, who do you and should you open up to? This is an even more important issue. Pay attention!

10. Have Stable and Genuine Relationships: It could be companionship, a relationship, or platonic friendship. It can be whatever you want, but the most important thing it should be is genuine – friendships with people who can understand your sensitivity and help you work with it are ideal. You know this. You know those who are truly and genuinely connected to you and care about you. It could be your parents, best friend, romantic partner, companion, sibling, or a relative; it's important to have someone who respects you and how you feel, and who won't make you feel bad for feeling the way you do. Someone who sees the wonderful and positive sides, even if he or she is not a highly sensitive person.

11. Find Quiet Time Alone: Taking time out to enjoy time alone is underestimated. As someone with sensory processing sensitivity and a hyper nervous system, you need time alone to examine yourself and converse with yourself. There's a need to create time to calm your nerves, reflect, and process things carefully. You need time to see your environment, think about your experiences, and create amazing things while occupying your own space. This uninterrupted alone-time gives your mind time to fill with bright ideas, thoughts, and innovations to create mind-blowing solutions.

Another pro of spending time alone: you'll understand yourself better, leading to more rational decisions, helping prevent burn-out because you are giving yourself time to breathe before you get overly exhausted. It also helps you discover your own voice and use it more actively. It's a great way to exercise self-care.

12. Channel Your Energy and Emotions into Creative Activities: Your sensitive nature can make your feelings seem overwhelming. Have you ever thought of putting these overwhelming feelings to better use? You can get a conglomeration of your feelings, thoughts, imaginations, experiences, and express them in whatever way you want to get them out of your system. It could be vocally, it could be through art, writing, painting, or drawing. Doing something worthwhile with your time makes you feel a sense of validation and achievement and preserves your self-esteem. Your ability to actively sense things/people around you (compared to non-HSPs) is a privilege and leverage that should not be treated lightly. Get creative; get going!

13. Food: Eat nutritious meals and drink lots of water; the importance of food cannot be overemphasized. Feeding your body well is vital for good health and strength, and water is beneficial to stay hydrated. The Hypersensitive person needs this even more. The fast-paced and higher frequency reaction to stimuli makes them get angry, irritable, or exhausted when hungry or dehydrated. Note this and take good care of yourself before the hungry HSP becomes the "hangry" HSP.

15. Know What Works for You and What Doesn't: Doing a serious self-assessment to learn what works for you – and what doesn't – is paramount to living a happy life; even more so to the HSP. There will also be situation and people you've seen (and that you are cool with) and situation/people you find unacceptable. Examine yourself to discover how parties make you feel. How much effect does noise or loud music have on you? What does socializing mean to you? Closely examining yours likes and dislikes offers you the option to weight options carefully *before* getting into situations that make you irritable or unhappy. You'll know how much work you can do at a time, if you can endure loud music or not, and if you are fine sharing experiences with someone else. You also know if you are okay with impromptu arrangements and you react to drinking (and drunks!) Understanding the environments in which you thrive – or don't – is key to recognizing people and environments that threaten your peace of mind. Notably, these people or things do not necessarily have to be bad, they may simply not be in tandem with your energy; that's fine, but you must handle it either way, keeping your space clear of any personal toxicity.

The HSP is bountifully blessed, and there are abundant tips to help you thrive and help you take care of yourself, making the best use of your sensitivity. Three major ways to offload your stress are:

- Through nature (taking a walkout, swimming, forest bathing, stargazing)
- Through the expression of creativity
- Through letting it out (vulnerability)

Remember always that you have control over your life and keeping away from triggers that may make you too overloaded is a good idea. If you list these things that send you into overdrive, you can use that list to decide what is and what is not acceptable in your life, and this makes your life much easier to handle.

Chapter 11: Tapping into The Hidden Power of HSP

You are a superhero of sorts. Not a superman who is well seen and works in the open, but more like a batman who operates in the dark but is very effective. Your senses, like a magnet, are attracted to and hooked by detail. They are more sensitive to happenings around you, and you feel much deeper than non-HSPs do. This can be a disadvantage if not properly used, but a huge asset if channeled the right way. A proper appreciation, followed by proper use of this trait's powers, is highly effective in different situations from the workplace setting to school, to general well-being as it has been emphasized that the personality trait is huge leverage.

One of the HSP's personality traits is the ability to pay great attention to detail. This ability, that many people may call Obsessive-Compulsive Disorder, can be harnessed into making amazing things of yourself, of your moments, imaginations, experiences, and those around you. Creativity is ignited and inspired more in hypersensitive people than in non-HSPs. Invariably, this results in a blast of talents woven into amazing works (most times, in the field of art). Such a great talent harnessed properly can cause one being good at detailed painting, drawing, writing (with emphasis on creative writing), carving, and even most types of artwork. Hypersensitivity is power, and it's difficult to harness most of the time. Sensitivity makes you feel bare, feel real, and feel open, making you want to resist your sensitive reality because you probably feel weakened by it. It screams for you not to resist it, but harness it and create the most mind-blowing things by using the power that comes with it. What power?

One major feature easily noticeable in HSPs is the tendency to enjoy solitude, and in that alone holds a huge power. There's power in coming together to achieve something. Still, when it comes to personal brainstorming and planning, especially when creating something artistic or creative, solitude carries a lot of power. There's something about that tendency that has a host of advantages. Below are the hidden powers of the Highly Sensitive Person.

1. Prevents Socialization Induced Distractions: One major power you have is that you prefer to be alone most of the time to think, observe, work things out and get things done. This helps in conserving time and sustaining the positive energy of being comfortable in your skin. You are also more likely to appreciate mother-nature and the aesthetic value of things. You'll also find that you are usually kinder to nature and treat her better. You can maximize time for yourself, for self-care, and for other tasks you must attend to. Many people in relationships have never experienced that power of being alone. At the end of a relationship, they feel incomplete. When you know the power of being you, you give yourself personal strength and a great sense of self-confidence.

2. Thinks Deeply and Critically Analyzes People and Situations: Hypersensitivity allows you to see and take in details and appropriately use this information. This personality trait also allows you to observe people and analyze situations through the removal of unwanted external stimuli. This makes you a deeper thinker with a better eye for detail than the average person. You are more likely to spot the person with the odd shoe in the room or the person who's sad but camouflaging it with a smile on his or her face. You are also most likely to spot individuals who are not genuine in relationships around you, but your empathetic spirit might find it hard to get rid of people just like that. Being sensitive is a huge power, and when properly used, it works for the greater good.

3. Excellent at Teamwork: When taking good care of yourself, validating yourself, and investing time and energy into things that matter, you can grow self-love. This self-love grooms self-development and growth, making personal goals attainable and helping to maximize talents and abilities. Ironically, since they are mostly associated with aloneness and solitude, it might be thought they might not do well as part of a team. The shock? They are far more likely to do better on a team than non-HSPs. Look at it this way. They are more sensitive. They can do things quicker and more thoroughly and come up with smart ideas and creations from their imaginations, observations, and quick attraction to detail. They understand the team members and give them chances to thrive because of their highly empathetic, sensitive, and understanding nature. You are likely to do well as a team member, especially in a field that involves gauging of feelings of others, such as in charity organizations and humanitarian outfit but taking a decision or high-pressure role might pose a problem.

4. Creative: Your imagination and creativity have a spark. Sensitivity ignites you with a passion for creating, especially when in an environment filled with inspiration. Feeling things and emotions even when others cannot is great leverage for you and channeling it in the proper direction is what makes it powerful. From the tangible and intangible, you can visualize and then create.

5. Creates Deep Relationships: This is because of the hypersensitive nature of your emotions and reaction to stimuli. You can understand others even before they explain to you what is going on. There's a huge empathetic behavior ingrained in your personality trait and putting it to good use can help you build strong and powerful bonds and relationships. It can be compared to having a lens to see through people. How powerful is that? You are highly empathetic and sensitive to people and the environment. You are a more considerate lover, friend, and colleague and can relate to and share in the misery of others as you can imagine what it feels like to be in their shoes. This makes for a more dependable and amiable personality in general.

6. Adaptable: Centuries ago, all dogs belonged in the wild. Then came man, who tamed them. They took them from the wilds and brought them into a new environment. Dogs got to see man's environment and then gradually adapted. Adaptability is an essential characteristic of not just animals, but all living things. This quality is more potent, as you are more likely to take time to see and internalize the environment. You are a master adaptor – a very useful skill applicable in all facets of life, observing and adapting quickly.

7. Highly Empathetic and Supportive: Wouldn't you call the ability to feel so deeply and intensely what you and others around you feel a superpower? It's something that makes up your unique mind and caring and understanding nature. Being empathetic helps you build strong relationships with people around you and places you as an excellent team player and leader. Compassion is a gift that the world needs; seeing someone who can give it readily is another gift. It's already a plus! Your job is to prove how much you are worth by wielding your abilities properly. By doing this, you can build strong bonds, help with advice, offer help to others, and even learn more about yourself and others and the human mind in general. There's fulfillment in offering help, care, love, guidance, or one form of support or another when people need them. One key way to maximize this power is by taking self-care seriously and not neglecting your own self-care by becoming overwhelmed by handling other people's issues. The sensitivity trait helps you understand people more and relate to them better.

8. Tendency to Become a Good Leader and Parent: The ability to think fast, observe, care about others, think well, and think creatively all made up in one person is a huge quality. You can make decisions while considering what your co-workers, followers, students, children, clients, or team members will feel. Only a few individuals can do that, but your sensitive ability supports that. The deal is about using it effectively. Your sensitive nature comes with disadvantages that can interfere in your life and may even cause a rough patch for you. Remember, you are taking on board a lot of emotions. Knowing how to balance things up will save you from becoming overwhelmed. What do I mean by disadvantages? In an instance where you lead a group of people on a particular project, there may be someone on that team that seems to want to take advantage of your sensitivity at every chance he or she gets. He or she constantly makes false excuses to skip work and duties because of the knowledge you are sensitive and most likely to believe him or her. They also know you will feel concerned, show concern, and allow his or her absence from work and will take advantage. What do you do in such a case? The same sensitivity that makes you feel concerned for people is the same sensitivity that will help you to discover if someone is genuine or not. You just need to pay attention and balance sensitivity and rationality to achieve the best results. Be empathetic but give yourself a voice too.

9. How Does Your Sensitivity Make You a Good Leader? You are emotionally intelligent. The ability to read other's minds and emotions should not be underrated. Invariably, they dare not be underrated. You can see and understand what or how people feel and know what they think even before asking or having them speak their minds. An emotionally intelligent leader, partner, parent, or team member will gain the trust, support, and confidence of others. The people you lead will understand that you show care and concern toward them and that you will understand when they come to you with suggestions, comments, worries, fears, or anything that could develop in your relationship with them. They can open up more to you and get your commiseration, felicitations, solidarity, agreement, or correction. You'll build a trust-filled, open-door relationship, and that's a healthy way forward for any relationship that wants growth. When things go wrong, they can help you assess situations. They can speak freely with you, reciprocate concern toward you too, and do work even more effectively and efficiently. As a hypersensitive person, you can notice, care, feel, understand, interpret, and create from these assets. You are powerful, and you can use that power to make great things happen that people will appreciate and be impressed by.

The powers that place you as more valuable than others are:

- Ability to observe even the tiniest details
- Emotional intelligence
- Great communication skills
- Problem-solving skills (creativity)

All leverages mentioned above are not purely refined bonuses that come with being hypersensitive; rather, you must build them. You'll need to wield them. You have the power, but you must learn to use it. In tapping into your hidden powers, you must also note there has to be a balance, so you don't hurt yourself or others or getting overwhelmed. Prepare mentally and emotionally for impromptu arrangements or unexpected circumstances, so you don't get caught off-guard and have to render your abilities as irrelevant. Finding a balance will help you navigate through the disadvantages that come with this power. See your sensitivity as to what it is—your greatest power! Sensitivity is only a problem if we approach it with a mindset it is. It's all about the mindset. Acknowledging, appreciating, and using the power of sensitivity is what makes it a power!

Chapter 12: The HSPs Contribution

Why are You so Important in the World?

HSPs have innumerable contributions to add and impact on making in and beyond the society in which they find him/herself. HSPs are about 15-20% of the world's population. It's little wonder why several people do not understand what it takes to be highly sensitive, why hypersensitive people are wired the way they are, or even what it means to be highly sensitive. Others mistake the sensitivity trait as a sort of weakness or inadequacy. Meanwhile, the irony is that hypersensitive people are the ones who even help non-hypersensitive people the most. Hypersensitivity is a unique personality trait, and it takes understanding from others that sensitivity is not a weakness for a hypersensitive person to thrive. It should be thought of as a strength. When other people are understanding, acknowledging, and accepting, they can properly wield the traits to achieve the best results. Knowing that hypersensitivity is a powerful trait is not enough to make an impact. Using it is what makes the impact. However, what are the contributions you must make or add? To have a full grasp on that, let's do a quick self-examination.

1. Have you, at any point, been labeled as being weak for being sensitive? Later, has your sensitivity made you offer help to that same person who labeled you as weak?

2. Have you been able to offer aid, advice, comfort, concern, or support of any sort to someone just by being emotionally intelligent and sensing something was wrong with them and offering to help?

3. Have you been able to help anybody be more open with their emotions or realize who they are by simply caring, listening, and being empathetic?

4. Have you, through your hypersensitivity, created a masterpiece (work of art) by simply weaving your feelings and observations into awesome expression?

5. Have you ever been able to feel things so deeply and intensely that you navigate your way through life and help people navigate their way through life simply by paying attention?

There are multitudes of questions and multitudes of answers to be examined, but since the aim is to drive home a point, let's delve into "The Highly Sensitive Person's Contribution."

Something was mentioned about hypersensitive people being the ones to help those who are not hypersensitive – contrary to the myth they are too emotional and weak and therefore need help. You are wondering how they can offer help. They experience emotional stimuli at a rate much faster than non-HSPs. You can feel things happening or something about to happen from a distance. When something happens, when sounds are made, when something goes wrong with someone else, you feel it deeper and faster, and this makes everybody wonder why you are made like this. You help them feel what the world is through your extra powerful lenses and senses. When your friend gets in trouble, and you get panicky and emotional, people wonder why you even feel the emotions more intensely than this person. The simple answer to these questions is that you feel you care, and you help. Hypersensitive people are wired to be more emotional, caring, and concerned about others even more than themselves sometimes. They are deeply concerned about their environment, nature, and everything that comes together to form this world. Therefore, you, as an HSP, will discover that you constantly want to express yourself. Searching, writing, painting, helping, and these elements put together to influence your growth as an individual because there's fulfillment you feel in expression, and that includes LENDING A HELPING HAND and or MAKING SOMETHING SPECIAL.

Check out most people who turn out to be:

1. Psychologists

2. Teachers

3. Counselors

4. Creatives (writers and artists)

5. Great parents

Guess what? They are HSPs! Because they connect to the world on a more intimate level and search fervently for a means to let out their findings from their connection with the world. They can relate to how and what the human mind feels like because they have been stuck there more often than not. You have swam up the shores from the depths of your mind when you fell into one phase of intense emotion. You know what it feels like as you have been there (it's more like you are always going there), plus you have a super ability to relate to others and understand them. A combination of these two results in you reading people, understanding them, and even guiding them through troubled times.

Highly Sensitive Persons make great teachers because of their empathetic nature and ability to connect and relate to others.

Counselors are usually HSPs, too, because, just like you, they have dealt with different phases of their lives (especially during the phase of life where misconstruing what sensitivity meant). Through certain trying phases, they know what it feels like to be lost, sad, depressed, and confused. They have needed a guide too, and they found one.

Sensitivity ignites creativity, awakens your senses to the reality of life and even the fantasy of life. It sparks imagination and the zeal to create. The most intense emotions arouse your senses to create something and even further ignite your passion for expressing yourself from the awareness of what is around you and the emotions that surround you. From these, you are not only creating simply to create, but to create great work.

What makes them great parents? They have empathy, emotional intelligence, good leadership skills, and the ability to connect with other humans so intensely. All the features that characterize them are invariably what makes them great parents. The few points enumerated above shed light on how much value you have to contribute to the world at large, not just for now but from generation to generation. Affecting lives through therapy, parenting, creativity, counseling, leadership, relationships, and being wired to be a good human generally are more than enough contributions to the world we live in. That's not all. There are more contributions to be made:

- Volunteering service to humanity

- Relationship Bonds

- Helping people to be more open and teaching others how to connect with themselves

This chapter subtly addressed what you offer as an HSP. It addressed what benefits abound in your sensitivity traits, what sensitivity offers you as a creative person (as a painter, a writer, etc.), and how you notice things when everybody else can't (at home, in the workplace and as a leader). You know how to influence people and open them to their vulnerability, teach people how to connect with their hearts, minds, and self and bring something beautiful out of it all, to themselves and the world and how this amounts to contribution upon contribution.

We live in a world that is harsh and unforgiving, with a lot of "lovelessness." You are among the amazing few with a lot of love to go round. This quality makes ideal parents, and in a world where parenting is increasingly challenging, HSPs make good, considerate parents as they can mentally connect with their children and shower them with love unconditionally. As a highly sensitive individual, parenting and guidance are likely to be your forte, and the world relies on people like you to make it a more compassionate and understanding place to be.

Having pointed out the leverages and benefits they have, it is pertinent to examine many challenges faced within a world filled with people who do not understand sensitivity. Some of these challenges include:

1. Being a Lone Ranger in a Complex World: Walking alone helps you to internalize happenings in your surroundings and to think and formulate new ideas. Most of all, you know how to generate inspiration and enjoy life's intensity. This is what the trait of sensitivity offers them. Sadly, with society and its ideologies portraying sensitivity to be a weakness, others do not always see you for your value. The difficulty in understanding how to treat, understand, or relate to HSPs has become a big deal.

Therefore, because others do not understand them, they leave them (the sensitive ones) to their dream world. They sometimes even make them feel less significant, weak, or ask, "Why are you like this?" The sensitive individual might then grow up to be accustomed to being a loner, although it may be good for enjoying the intensity of life, exploring solo, and creating finding new ideas.

This makes them socially awkward and secluded so that when they grow up, it still affects them and their social mentality. If care is not taken, they might become loners for all their lives and eventually become depressed or socially awkward.

2. Lack of Understanding: If all HSPs were asked a universal question, "What do you wish was different about how you were treated when younger?" most will reply with "I wish that they had understood me." Showing sensitivity to the plights of highly sensitive persons will help you – and others – to understand them better and treat them better. Consider what they feel, and include them in decision-making processes. We need more caring and sensitive people in this world – not more people who see sensitivity as abnormal and insignificant.

3. The Surprised Looks: As an HSP in a world dominated by insensitive people, you automatically are tasked with having to downplay your reactions to things the insensitive individuals perceive as normal. Your reaction to many of these scenarios might cause a questioning look from those around you, and that might present an awkward situation. You must face this; prepare for surprised looks when you react differently to certain things. It's the viewer's weakness, *not yours.*

4. Being Labeled Anti-social or Boring: HSPs naturally avoid a lot of things because of their highly stimulated response system, being labeled anti-social due to their preference for solitary moments. When an HSP is around family and friends, this trait is even more magnified. Remember, those quiet moments are important to you and to your health.

5. You May Pry: Due to your highly sensitive nature, you often know people's thoughts, feelings, and moods. Your friendly and caring nature might make you ask questions, hoping to help the person ease their problems. Although you might read expressions incorrectly, your questions and curiosity about what is wrong with a friend might be seen as prying. You find it hard to let go of your thoughts about the feelings of perplexed or troubled people, and anytime you try to let go, your conscience most probably hunts you down and propels you into going back to make sure that person is okay.

Often, HSPs are targets for relationship advice or general life advice because others do come to them for help about their lives. Yet, when it's time for an HSP to face their demons, there seems to be no one around. You may listen to other people's problems, but you should never forget that you also have your own to deal with.

On a final note, you deserve to be respected. You hold a position and always contribute your intellect and innovative ideas to developing whatever situation you find yourself in. HSPs rarely are noticed immediately in an environment. Their quiet and mild nature does not give way for a popular presence in an environment. Rather, they are spotted when contributing to ideas or solving a general problem, but it may later be revealed that their distance from the situation was for a very good purpose.

Speak up when decisions are made *for* you that don't take into consideration your interests. Otherwise, you may be playing into the hands of bullies and manipulator.

Your high sensitivity is undoubtedly a blessing; still, remember that most great things don't come easily. Standing up to bullies and these conditions is a challenge, but also the way to secure your position and the respect that goes along with it.

Not everybody will understand your personality or why you seem undecided about things. Everyone thinks differently. Once you've arrived at your decision – or even at a suggestion – boldly move forward and support it. If you consistently come off as weak (or silent), people will no longer seek your opinions. When you *do* voice them, expect the respect that comes from being a different voice and a kinder opinion.

Conclusion

HSPs have much more to gain and give to their environment while maintaining a sane and healthy lifestyle. Having considered the several common traits and possible feelings you experience as a highly sensitive person (as well as new ways to react to the situations it creates), you are more than ready to establish a new you – a "you" that better relates to people around you and perceives situations in a healthy way, free from overthinking and other mentally draining habits.

Consider and reconsider the insights provided here, cutting across several aspects of human life - like pets, nature, parenting, and children.

Now that you better understand HSPs and how others perceive them, you can adjust your behavior and reactions, knowing that you are indeed a special person with much to offer those you meet. Also, rest assured that your insights and sensitivities are a blessing – not a curse. Use them wisely!

Here's another book by Mari Silva that you might like

MARI SILVA

Advanced Reiki Healing

Enhance Your Skills in Reiki Healing, Symbol Activations, Distance Healing, Angelic Reiki, Crystal Healing, and More

Your Free Gift (only available for a limited time)

Thanks for getting this book! If you want to learn more about various spirituality topics, then join Mari Silva's community and get a free guided meditation MP3 for awakening your third eye. This guided meditation mp3 is designed to open and strengthen ones third eye so you can experience a higher state of consciousness. Simply visit the link below the image to get started.

https://spiritualityspot.com/meditation

References

10 Life-Changing Tips for Highly Sensitive People. (2015, July 23). Marc and Angel Hack Life. https://www.marcandangel.com/2015/07/22/10-life-changing-tips-for-highly-sensitive-people/

Best Careers for Introverts, HSPs, and Other Sensitive Souls | Val Nelson. (2018, April 11). Valnelson.com. https://valnelson.com/introvert-power/best-careers-for-introverts-hsps-and-other-sensitive-souls/

Brooks, H. (2020, June 29). *19 Ways Being a Highly Sensitive Person Affects Your Love Life.* IntrovertDear.com. https://introvertdear.com/news/highly-sensitive-person-relationships-affects/

Elaine. (2016, February 25). *Suicide and High Sensitivity – The Highly Sensitive Person.* Hsperson.com. https://hsperson.com/suicide-and-high-sensitivity/

Highly Sensitive People Can Change The World — If We Let Them. (2015, August 6). The Odyssey Online. https://www.theodysseyonline.com/highly-sensitive-people-change-world

How Highly Sensitive People Can Change the World for the Better. (2016, July 12). My Libertarian Lifestyle. https://mylibertarianlifestyle.wordpress.com/2016/07/12/how-highly-sensitive-people-can-change-the-world-for-the-better/

How to Help Highly Sensitive Employees Thrive. (2015, December 8). The Good Men Project. https://goodmenproject.com/featured-content/how-to-help-highly-sensitive-employees-thrive-dsh/

Is Your Child Highly Sensitive? – The Highly Sensitive Person. (n.d.). Hsperson.com. Retrieved from https://hsperson.com/test/highly-sensitive-child-test/

January 26, dancingmoonlavendar, & Pm, 2017 at 11:13. (2016, April 11). *Empath Or Highly Sensitive: Which One Do You Think You Are?* Mind Journal. https://themindsjournal.com/are-you-an-empath-or-hsp/

jenngranneman. (2019, December 13). *21 Signs You're a Highly Sensitive Person.* Highly Sensitive Refuge. https://highlysensitiverefuge.com/highly-sensitive-person-signs/

May. 31, S. A. |, & 2020. (2020, May 31). *The 10 Best Dogs for Highly Sensitive People.* PureWow. https://www.purewow.com/wellness/dogs-for-highly-sensitive-people

Psychology Today Canada: Health, Help, Happiness + Find a Therapist CA. (2019). Psychology Today. https://www.psychologytoday.com

Renzi, M. N. (2017, August 7). *8 Special Superpowers of Highly Sensitive People.* Melissa Noel Renzi. https://melissanoelrenzi.com/highly-sensitive-people-superpowers/

Romantic Relationships with a Highly Sensitive Person (HSP). (2016, November 4). Exploring Your Mind. https://exploringyourmind.com/romantic-relationships-highly-sensitive-person-hsp/

Schwanke, C. (n.d.). *Careers for Highly Sensitive People.* LoveToKnow. Retrieved from https://jobs.lovetoknow.com/careers-highly-sensitive-people

Tanaaz. (2015, May 22). *Are You An Empath or Just Highly Sensitive?* Forever Conscious. https://foreverconscious.com/are-you-an-empath-or-just-highly-sensitive

The 5 greatest tips for highly sensitive people to thrive in life. (n.d.). Hisensitives.com. Retrieved from https://hisensitives.com/the-5-greatest-tips-for-highly-sensitive-people-to-thrive-in-life/

The 7 Best Careers for a Highly Sensitive Person. (2018, August 8). Highly Sensitive Refuge. https://highlysensitiverefuge.com/highly-sensitive-person-careers/

The Difference between HSP, Empath, & Clairsentient. (2016, October 19). Jennifer Soldner. http://www.jennifersoldner.com/2016/10/hsp-empath-or-clairsentient.html

The Differences Between Highly Sensitive People and Empaths. (n.d.). Psychology Today. Retrieved from https://www.psychologytoday.com/us/blog/the-empaths-survival-guide/201706/the-differences-between-highly-sensitive-people-and-empaths

THE PROS AND CONS OF BEING HIGHLY SENSITIVE. (2015, October 22). The Daily Guru. https://www.thedailyguru.com/being-highly-sensitive/

The Special Connection Between Highly Sensitive Kids and Pets. (2019, January 2). Highly Sensitive Refuge. https://highlysensitiverefuge.com/highly-sensitive-children-pets/

Understanding highly sensitive children. (n.d.). Focus on the Family. Retrieved from https://www.focusonthefamily.ca/content/understanding-highly-sensitive-children

Zinc Deficiency And The Highly Sensitive Person. (2017, April 3). Journey Thru Wellness. http://journeythruwellness.com/zinc-deficiency-highly-sensitive-person/

11 Types of Empaths – Which Type of Empath Am I? (2019, December 6). Insight state website: https://www.insightstate.com/spirituality/types-of-empaths/

Allie. (2012, October 9). Is empathy a weakness? Allie Creative website: http://alliecreative.com/2012/is-empathy-a-weakness/

Brallier, S. (2020, January 30). What Are the Pros and Cons of Being an Empath? Learn Religions website

Amanda, B. (2020, June 30). 8 Major Downsides to Being an Empath. Exemplore website

Burn, S. (2019, June 19). Is Empathy Your Greatest Strength and Greatest Weakness? Psychology Today website

Flaker, A. (2016, February 9). *5 Painful Pitfalls of Being an Empath.* Chakra Center website: https://chakracenter.org/2016/02/09/5-painful-pitfalls-of-being-an-empath/

Gourley, C. (2020). ASCENSION, THE NEW EARTH, AND THE ROLE OF THE EMPATH [YouTube Video]. https://www.youtube.com/watch?v=jbGDmSyA-Ks

Heights, A. (2016, October 5). The Pitfalls Of Anger For The Empath. psychicbloggers.com website

Hurd, S. (2018, June 22). The Truth about Empaths and Relationships That No One Talks about. Life Advancer website: https://www.lifeadvancer.com/truth-empaths-and-relationships/

How The Full Moon Affects Your Energy and Emotions As An Empath – True Empath. (n.d.). https://www.trueempath.com/full-moon-and-empaths/

Judith, O. (n.d.). 10 Traits Empathic People Share. Psychology Today website

Markowitz, D. (2017, October 28). The Best Diet for Empaths and Highly Sensitive Persons. Self-Care for the Self-Aware website: https://www.davemarkowitz.com/blog.php?article=Diet-for-Empaths-and-Highly-Sensitive-Persons_36

Michaela. (2017, March 13). THE BEST DIET FOR INTROVERTS? Surprising Links Between Personality & Food. Introvert Spring website: https://introvertspring.com/best-introvert-diet/

Michaela. (2019, August 6). How to Create an Empath Friendly Home. Introvert Spring website: https://introvertspring.com/how-to-create-an-empath-friendly-home/

Orloff, J. (2017, April 20). The Power of Being an Earth Empath. Elephant Journal website: https://www.elephantjournal.com/2017/04/the-power-of-being-an-earth-empath/

Orloff, J. (2019, March 19). Are you a Food Empath? 6 Strategies to Overcome Food Addictions & Overeating. Elephant Journal website: https://www.elephantjournal.com/2019/03/are-you-a-food-empath-6-strategies-to-overcome-food-addictions-overeating-judith-orloff/

Orloff, J. (2017, June 3). The Differences Between Empaths and Highly Sensitive People. Judith Orloff MD website: https://drjudithorloff.com/the-difference-between-empaths-and-highly-sensitive-people/

Robertson, R. (2016, March 17). The Strength of Empathy. Key Person of Influence website: http://www.keypersonofinfluence.com/the-strength-of-empathy/

Rodriguez, D. (2009, May 20). How To Lead a Well-Balanced Life. EverydayHealth.com website

Sinclair, G. (2017, November 3). 8 Untold Strengths All Empaths Have. Awareness Act website: https://awarenessact.com/8-untold-strengths-all-empath-have/

The 10 Big Benefits Of Being An Empath. (2019, June 12). In5D website: https://in5d.com/10-empath-benefits/

The Differences Between Empaths and Highly Sensitive People. (2017, June 3). Judith Orloff MD website: https://drjudithorloff.com/the-difference-between-empaths-and-highly-sensitive-people/

This is How Empaths Are Affected by Natural Disasters | Whole Secrets. (2017, September 25). wholesecrets.com website: https://wholesecrets.com/this-is-how-empaths-are-affected-by-natural-disasters/

What are the strengths of an empath? - Quora. (n.d.).

What Is An Empath? 15 Signs and Traits. (2019, November 25). Healthline website: https://www.healthline.com/health/what-is-an-empath#deep-caring

Winter, C. (2018, February 20). 6 Reasons Why Empaths May Struggle With Their Weight. A Conscious Rethink website: https://www.aconsciousrethink.com/7314/6-reasons-empaths-particularly-prone-weight-issues/

Winter, C. (2018, December 10). 9 Reasons Why Empaths Love Nature So Much. A Conscious Rethink website: https://www.aconsciousrethink.com/9412/empaths-in-nature/

Wolfe, D. (2016, April 27). Are You An Empath? THIS is the Type of Relationship You Want to Be In! David Avocado Wolfe website: https://www.davidwolfe.com/empath-relationship-want-to-be-in/

Wong, A. (2008, August). Have a Balanced Lifestyle. wikiHow website

Van Kimmenade, C. (2014, July 22). 7 Phases of Becoming a Skilled Empath. The Happy Sensitive website: https://thehappysensitive.com/7-phases-of-becoming-skilled-empath/

Valentine, M. (2018, April 18). Here Are the Biggest Pros and Cons of Being an Empath. Goalcast website: https://www.goalcast.com/2018/04/18/pros-cons-being-an-empath/

Victor Hansen, M. (2011, February 3). How to Create a Balanced Life: 9 Tips to Feel Calm and Grounded. Tiny Buddha website: https://tinybuddha.com/blog/9-tips-to-create-a-balanced-life/